INDIANAPOLIS

WHAT TO DO, WHERE TO GO, AND HOW TO HAVE FUN IN INDIANAPOLIS

by Layne Scott Cameron

John Muir Publications

Santa Fe, New Mexico

*To Sandy, Alex, and Kyle: the greatest
adventures of life will be with the people and
places you're closest to.*

John Muir Publications,
P.O. Box 613, Santa Fe, NM 87504

Copyright © 1997 by John Muir Publications
Cover and maps © 1997 by John Muir Publications
All rights reserved.

Printed in the United States of America
First edition. First printing April 1997

ISBN 1-56261-346-4 (pbk.)

Editors Dianna Delling, Lizann Flatt
Production Nikki Rooker
Graphics Stephen Dietz, Jane Susan MacCarter
Typesetting Kathleen Sparkes
Activities Bobi Martin
Cover Design Caroline Van Remortel
Cover Photo © Don Eastman
Back Cover Photo Mike Fender/Indianapolis Zoo
Illustrations Stacy Venturi-Pickett
Maps Susan Harrison
Printer Burton & Mayer, Inc.

Kidding Around is a registered trademark of
John Muir Publications.

Distributed to the book trade by
Publishers Group West
Emeryville, California

About the Author: Layne Scott Cameron is an
editor and freelance writer who is a native of
Indianapolis. He lives there with his wife, Sandy,
and two boys, Alex and Kyle. Layne is an
assistant editor for the *American Legion Magazine*,
contributes to many national children's and adult
magazines, and is the author of *Mountain Bike
Indiana* (Beachway Press, 1996). When not
writing, Layne can be found bicycling or spending
time outdoors with his family.

CONTENTS

COLOR THE ROUTE
FROM YOUR HOMETOWN
TO INDIANAPOLIS

If you're flying, color the states you'll fly over. If you're driving,
color the states you'll drive through. If you live in Indianapolis or Indiana,
color the states you have visited.

WELCOME TO INDIANAPOLIS!

WELCOME TO INDIANAPOLIS, THE CAPITAL OF INDIANA. Over the years, Indianapolis has been labeled with many nicknames. Indianapolis has been called the Crossroads of America for its many interstates and railroads. The circle at the center of town earned it the title Circle City. Sports lovers call it the Amateur Sports Capital of the World because it hosts many sporting events and is home to several sports governing bodies. Lots of people simply call it "Indy," for short.

Indianapolis sits along the White River.

People from Indiana and Indianapolis are nicknamed Hoosiers. Many tall tales have been used to explain the name's origin. One popular story has to do with a man named Hoosier. Hoosier was a contractor who worked on the Louisville and Portland canal. Most of the men in his work force were from Indiana. When these hearty rivermen came into town, the townspeople stated, "Here come Hoosier's men."

Indianapolis

A Capital Move

On December 11, 1816, Indiana became the Union's nineteenth state. The town of Corydon, along the Ohio River, was the first state capital. But within four years of statehood, the legislature decided to find a new capital with a central location.

Their search brought them to Fall Creek Settlement—a trading post at the branches of Fall Creek and the West Fork of the White River. The site offered a natural waterway, fertile land, and a central location. Picking the site was easy, but giving it a name was not. One statesman wanted to name the city Tecumseh, after the great Shawnee chief. After a lengthy debate, the Assembly finally agreed upon Indianapolis.

Indianapolis in the 1820s ⇡

Indiana Presidents

Benjamin Harrison served as the twenty-third president of the United States. But he wasn't the first in his family to hold this office. Benjamin's grandfather, William Henry Harrison, was the ninth president.

In 1960, Indianapolis resident Frank Beckwith became the first black candidate to run for president.

WELCOME TO

Maggieapolis

If you had a chance to rename the city of Indianapolis, what would you want to call it? Write your answer on the sign above. Why did you choose that name? Write your answer in the space below.

_____

_____

_____

_____

THE GREATEST SPECTACLE IN RACING

"Gentlemen, start your engines!" Year after year, since 1911, this famous statement has signaled the start of the Indianapolis 500—the greatest spectacle in racing. Imagine what it is like to travel around the famed 2½-mile oval at 230 miles per hour. Although the race covers 500 miles, at that speed it lasts just three hours!

The first drivers never imagined racing at speeds that high or finishing the race in such a short time. In fact, Ray Harroun, the first winner, won the race with an average speed of 74 miles per hour. Your parents have probably driven that fast on the interstate!

Danny Sullivan won the 1985 Indy 500 by spinning and winning. Trying to take the lead early in the race, Danny spun his car completely around but didn't wreck. He came into the pits, changed all four tires, and went on to win his first 500.

Indiana Pacer Reggie Miller

HOOSIER HYSTERIA

Professional or college games, high school or pickup games, Hoosiers are fanatical about basketball. Bobby Knight, Reggie Miller, Oscar Robertson, Isiah Thomas, George McGinnis, Glenn Robinson, and Larry Bird all have ties to Indiana.

Unofficially, Indiana has more basketball hoops per capita than any other state in the Union. Goals are mounted to telephone poles, the tops of garages, or the sides of barns. If it's ten feet tall, it probably has a rim and a net hanging from it.

ON THE MOVE

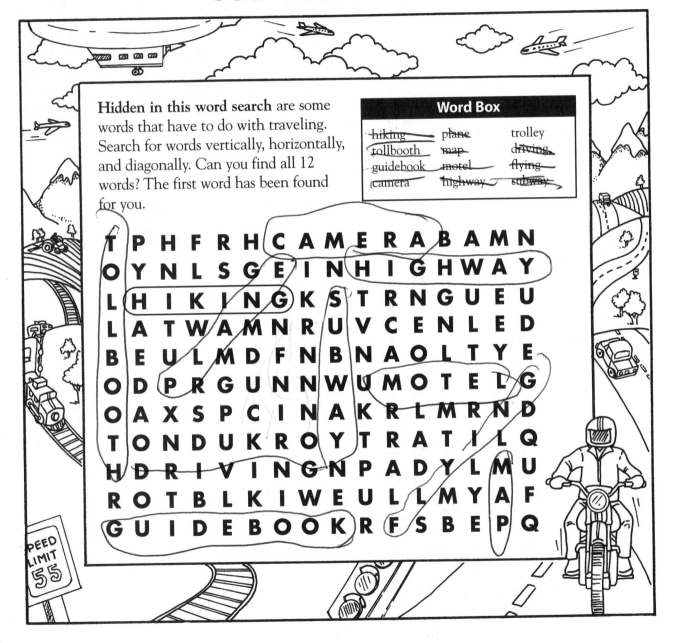

Hidden in this word search are some words that have to do with traveling. Search for words vertically, horizontally, and diagonally. Can you find all 12 words? The first word has been found for you.

Word Box

hiking	plane	trolley
tollbooth	map	driving
guidebook	motel	flying
camera	highway	subway

```
T P H F R H C A M E R A B A M N
O Y N L S G E I N H I G H W A Y
L H I K I N G K S T R N G U E U
L A T W A M N R U V C E N L E D
B E U L M D F N B N A O L T Y E
O O D P R G U N N W U M O T E L G
O A X S P C I N A K R L M R N D
T O N D U K R O Y T R A T I L Q
H D R I V I N G N P A D Y L M U
R O T B L K I W E U L L M Y A F
G U I D E B O O K R F S B E P Q
```

THE HOOSIER POET

You better mind yer parunts an'
  yer teachurs fond an' dear,
An churish them 'at loves you, an'
  dry the orphant's tear,
An he'p the pore an needy ones 'at
  clusters all about,
Er' the Gobble'uns'll git you ef
  you don't watch out!

↑ **James Whitcomb Riley**

Many an Indiana child quaked in their boots after hearing James Whitcomb Riley's tale of *Little Orphant Annie*. Many Indiana parents read the poem to teach their children proper manners.

Riley, known as the Hoosier Poet, was a master storyteller. He was best known for his children's poems like *Little Orphant Annie* and *The Raggedy Man*. Riley was a poet for grown-ups as well. As he traveled across the country, his recitals drew huge crowds. Here in Indianapolis, Riley read his poem *The Soldier* at the dedication of the Soldiers' and Sailors' Monument on the city's circle.

Raggedy Ann and Raggedy Andy dolls were based on characters from James Whitcomb Riley's poems.

DRAW YOUR OWN BUILDINGS

You're bound to see tall buildings in a city like Indianapolis. If you could draw a building of your own, what would it look like? Draw your buildings on this page, then color in the scene.

GAP-TOOTHED HOOSIER

It's no surprise that David Letterman, late-night funny man, made people laugh long before he was a talk show host. At his after-school job at Atlas Supermarket, David stacked a tower of canned corn from the floor to the ceiling. The cans were so tight that no one could pull out a single one.

As an adult, Dave's silly stunts got him fired from many jobs. Dave didn't change, though. He just kept looking for a job that was right for him. In California, Dave finally found a job that he couldn't get fired from: performing stand-up comedy and writing jokes for television sitcoms. His success at both led him to host his own show. The rest is "Late Night" history.

The Emmy Award–winning host of ⇑ *Late Night* comes from Indianapolis.

David Letterman once covered the Rose Bowl for an Indiana radio station. As a joke, he reported there was a shortage of roses that year and the floats were made of pork rinds.

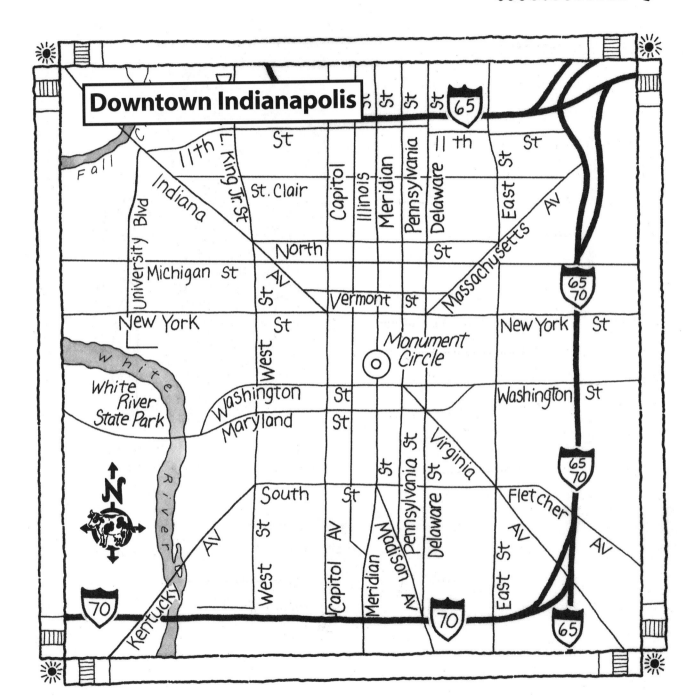

Downtown Indianapolis

WHAT TO WEAR

There's a saying that if you don't like the weather in Indianapolis, wait five minutes and it will change. The city's record high was 116 degrees Fahrenheit, while the all-time low was minus 35 degrees. In the summer, you can drench your shirt in sweat just by walking to your car in the humidity. In the winter, the wind chill can freeze your nose hairs in a matter of seconds. So, depending on what time of year it is, you'll need some tips on what to wear.

⬆ **Dress for warm weather if you're planning a summer trip to Indianapolis.**

IN THE SUMMER, BRING:

shorts, swimsuit, T-shirts, tank tops, sunscreen, water bottle, sunglasses, hat, beach towel, long socks (for skate rental), in-line skates, swim goggles, binoculars (for bird-watching), camera, and dress clothes

IN THE WINTER, BE SURE TO PACK:

long pants, flannel shirts, sweatshirts, insulated underwear, two pairs of shoes, swimsuit (indoor swimming), wool hat, scarf, gloves, lip balm, ice skates, camera, and dress clothes

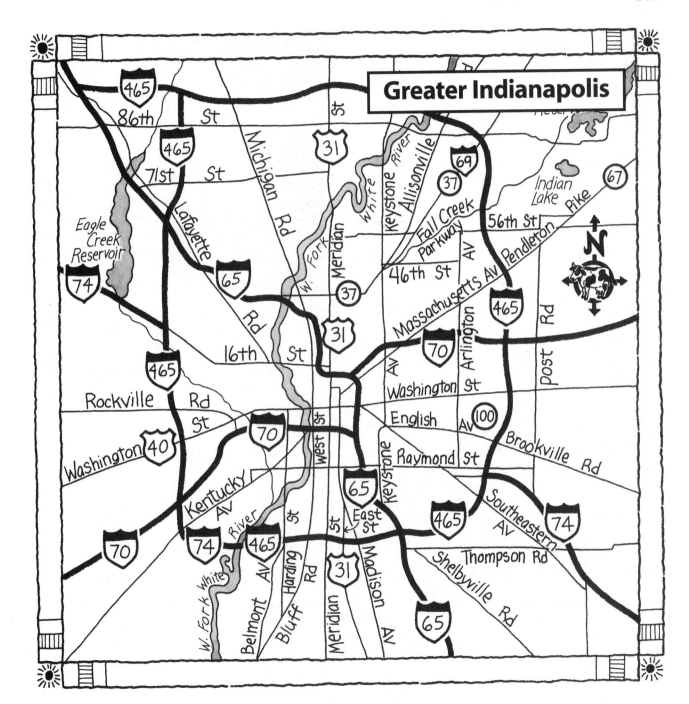

Greater Indianapolis

PARKS AND THE GREAT OUTDOORS

EVEN INDIANA'S CAPITAL CITY HAS ITS SHARE of outdoor activities. There are plenty of city parks and pools that offer year-round activities like swimming, fishing, and hiking. If you would rather learn about Johnny Appleseed and agriculture, check out Adrian Orchard or Stonycreek Farm. The folks there can show you how to grow apples and how to pick out the best pumpkin. On the north side of the Indianapolis Zoo, the River Promenade serves as a tribute to Indiana limestone. See how many famous buildings you can find that were built with Indiana stone. Whatever your choice, leave the asphalt and the traffic behind and enjoy the great outdoors in Indianapolis.

Autumn hayrides are offered at Eagle Creek Park.

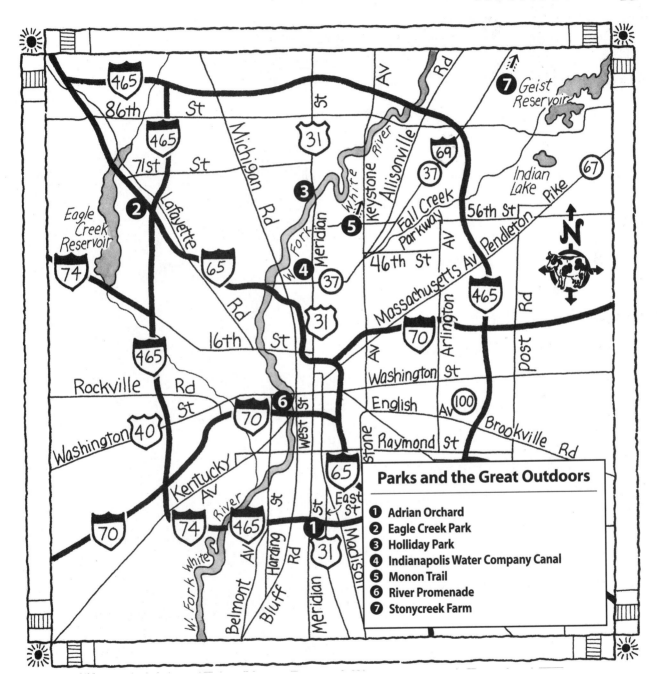

Parks and the Great Outdoors

1. Adrian Orchard
2. Eagle Creek Park
3. Holliday Park
4. Indianapolis Water Company Canal
5. Monon Trail
6. River Promenade
7. Stonycreek Farm

EAGLE CREEK PARK

In 1966, Indianapolis businessman J.K. Lilly donated his weekend retreat on Eagle Creek to the city. It was designated as a city park. Today Eagle Creek Park consists of 3,500 wooded acres surrounding a 1,300-acre reservoir that offers an activity for everyone.

Outdoor and fitness enthusiasts hike and jog on the miles of hiking trails that lace through the woods and around the main reservoir and two smaller lakes. Cyclists and in-line skaters pedal and glide around the paved 5 kilometer and 10 kilometer routes. Fishermen catch a variety of fish such as bass, bluegill, and catfish. The park also offers board sailing, canoe and paddleboat rentals, and a swimming beach.

⬆ **The trails at Eagle Creek are perfect for walking or jogging.**

Eagle Creek Park is the largest city-owned park in the United States.

COLOR TO FIND THE ANSWER

Creatures like these roam the bottom of the lakes in Eagle Creek Park!
Color the shapes with numbers blue. Color the shapes with letters orange.

INDIANAPOLIS WATER COMPANY CANAL

During the riverboat boom of the early 1800s, river towns bustled with people and businesses. In order to access the booming river towns, Indianapolis began construction on what was originally called the Central Canal. But bankruptcy and the development of the railroad kept the canal from being finished. Today what remains of the Indianapolis Water Company Canal is a 9-mile waterway that connects downtown Indianapolis with the village of Broad Ripple. Along its trail, you can jog, bike, or hike past many of the city's landmarks.

The trail begins at the Heslar Naval Armory and ends in Broad Ripple, within walking distance of many restaurants and unique shops. Along the way you'll pass Crown Hill Cemetery, the Indianapolis Museum of Art, and more.

⇑ **A trip down the canal takes you past many Indy landmarks.** ⇓

The Indianapolis Water Company Canal is the longest existing canal in the state.

LITTLE LOST TUG

Finish →

Start →

Can you help this tugboat find its way to the dock?

MONON TRAIL

"Rails to Trails" is a national campaign to convert abandoned railroad tracks into useful trails. In tribute to the Monon railway, a "train" of in-line skaters fly up the Monon Trail most Wednesdays at 5:30 p.m. If you want to join in but don't have your own skates, you can rent a pair at Sitzmark, near the north trailhead in Carmel.

If you would rather travel at a slower pace, hike or take a casual bicycle ride. The trail begins at 62nd Street in Broad Ripple and runs north to 86th Street in Nora. Someday the trail will stretch from 146th Street in Carmel to downtown Indianapolis.

⇑
Kids enjoy a riverside stroll.

⇐
Cyclists take in the area's scenic beauty.

Broad Ripple was named for the broad ripple at the bend in the White River.

WHAT'S THE DIFFERENCE

**These two pictures of in-line skaters might look the same, but they are not. How many differences between the two scenes can you find?
Hint: There are at least 15 differences.**

HOLLIDAY PARK

This park is named after John Holliday, founder of the *Indianapolis News*, one of the town's two daily newspapers. His 80-acre estate was donated to the city in 1916 to be used as a city park. The Hollidays even donated their house for use as a botanical garden.

⇡ *The Ruins* at Holliday Park

Today the park is known for its donated sculptures. The *Races of Man* were saved from a demolished building in New York City. Once they were moved to Indianapolis, three limestone tablets were added to the display to represent the three branches of government (executive, judiciary, and legislative), and the display was renamed *The Ruins*.

Along with sculptures, you'll find large flower gardens and hiking trails in the woods at the park. There are also picnic tables and playground equipment.

"Restore the Earth" day is an annual workday to rid the park of aliens— alien plants, that is. Volunteers protect native plants by weeding out alien plants like honeysuckle and garlic mustard.

⇐ **A gazebo welcomes visitors.**

WHICH ARE THE SAME?

Can you tell which two sculptures in the sculpture garden are exactly alike? When you've circled the sculptures that are the same, color in the scene.

CITY PARKS

Indianapolis has 140 city-owned parks and 12 city-owned golf courses. With so many places to choose from, it may be difficult to decide what to do first.

Many of the city's aquatic centers have Olympic-sized pools, diving boards, and water slides. With names like Roaring Rapids and Blue Wave, the slides are sure to provide a wet and wild day of fun.

Along with swimming, the parks offer dancing, martial arts, gymnastics, hockey, and a variety of other sports. Seasonal outdoor crafts and nature classes are also featured. "Grow Your Own Butterfly" teaches you about cocoons and flight, and "Nature Explorers" teaches you outdoor games. Call the Indianapolis Parks office for more information.

⬆ **Splishing and splashing at the Riverside Aquatic Center.**

In 1881, the Indianapolis park known as Bradley Woods was renamed Garfield Park following President James Garfield's assassination.

CROSSWORD FUN

ACROSS

2. This park was named for a president, not a cartoon cat.
4. This sport is played on an ice rink.
5. Professional athletes must do this to play well.
6. Indianapolis owns 140 of these.
8. In the "Grow Your Own _____" class you'll learn about cocoons and flight.
9. In sports, the team with the highest _____ wins.

DOWN

1. If you take your lunch to the park you can have one of these.
2. In this indoor sport you might use a balance beam or work on a tumbling routine.
3. Many pools in Indianapolis have one of these to jump from. (Hint: it's two words)
7. Blue Wave and Roaring Rapids are water _____.

Clue Box

butterfly   parks
diving board   train
Garfield   hockey
slides   gymnastics
score   picnic

ADRIAN ORCHARD

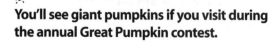

↑ Kids of all ages love apples.

McIntosh, Jonathan, Red Delicious, and Priscilla are all types of apples, and they can all be found at Adrian Orchard. In the fall, you can be part of an organized tour. The tour guides will lead you through the rows of fruit trees and teach you about pruning and how bees help apple trees grow. They will also teach you the proper way to pick an apple. With two twists and a quick flip, the apple snaps cleanly off the tree.

Back at the main building, you can buy bushels of apples and gallons of cider. The orchard is open from June to January, and sometimes longer if the season permits. Group tours are scheduled when the apples are ripe on the tree. Call the week after Labor Day to schedule a tour.

↑ You'll see giant pumpkins if you visit during the annual Great Pumpkin contest.

George Adrian holds the world record for most apples picked: 365½ bushels in eight hours.

HIDE AND SEEK

Draw circles around all 16 hidden objects in this picture.
When you're done, color in the scene. Look for: a cup, banana, paintbrush,
ruler, bell, duck head, baseball, rabbit face, ice cream cone, toothbrush,
face, baseball bat, wrench, candle, bucket, and grapes.

STONYCREEK FARM

Cool, crisp air and frost on the ground signal that it's time to head out to the pumpkin patch at Stonycreek Farm. What could be better than picking your own pumpkin?

As the wagon rolls out to the field, you can sing or stuff straw down your brother's shirt. But when the wagon wheels stop turning, you'd better be ready to find the biggest, roundest, most perfect pumpkin that you can carry.

The Halloween season is the busiest at the farm, but there are activities planned year-round. At Christmas, you and your family can pick out your own Christmas tree. In the summer, plan on playing volleyball, softball, or tramping along the fitness trail.

At Stonycreek, goats will eat right out of your hands.

PUMPKIN PATROL

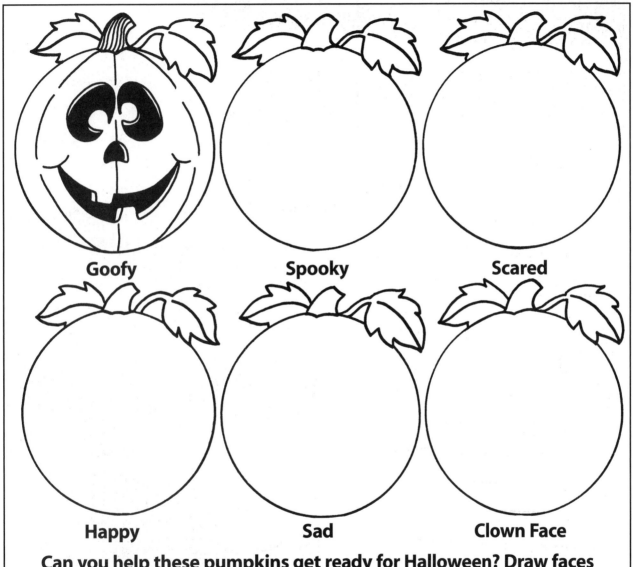

Goofy   Spooky   Scared

Happy   Sad   Clown Face

Can you help these pumpkins get ready for Halloween? Draw faces to match the word or words that appear below each pumpkin.

RIVER PROMENADE

A region in southern Indiana is known as Stone Country for its deposits of limestone. This high-grade stone has served as the building blocks for many famous buildings all over the country. The Empire State Building in New York City, the National Cathedral in Washington, D.C., and the Indiana State Capitol in Indianapolis were all built from Hoosier limestone.

Along the River Promenade's nature trail you can see miniature models of these buildings. The park is located on the north side of the Indianapolis Zoo on the bank of the White River.

You will also find inscriptions that tell how Indiana limestone was created. Stone benches provide a welcome break and offer a view of the downtown skyline.

Over 1,200 stones were donated to build the park. Each of them is the size of the refrigerator in your kitchen!

Stone lines the trail of the River Promenade.

MY TRAVEL JOURNAL
—Parks and the Great Outdoors—

I had fun when I visited: _____

I learned about: _____

My favorite park was: _____

What I enjoyed doing the most was: _____

This is a picture of what I saw at a park in Indianapolis

3 ANIMALS AROUND INDIANAPOLIS

ANIMALS CAN BE FOUND ALL AROUND INDIANAPOLIS— even right downtown. A wolf, a hawk, a heron, a skunk, or a blue-tailed skink might be closer than you think. At Wolf Park, you can learn to howl like a wolf. While walking downtown, you may see a peregrine falcon dive at top speed to knock down his prey. If you visit Eagle Creek Park, make sure to pack your binoculars. Thousands of birds migrate through Indiana each year and use the park as a stopover during their travels. And don't forget the Indianapolis Zoo. It's home to animals from all over the world, from sea lions to Siberian tigers and polar bears—oh, my! Grab your safari hat and see what you can find.

↑ Get a close-up view of swimming sharks at the Indianapolis Zoo.

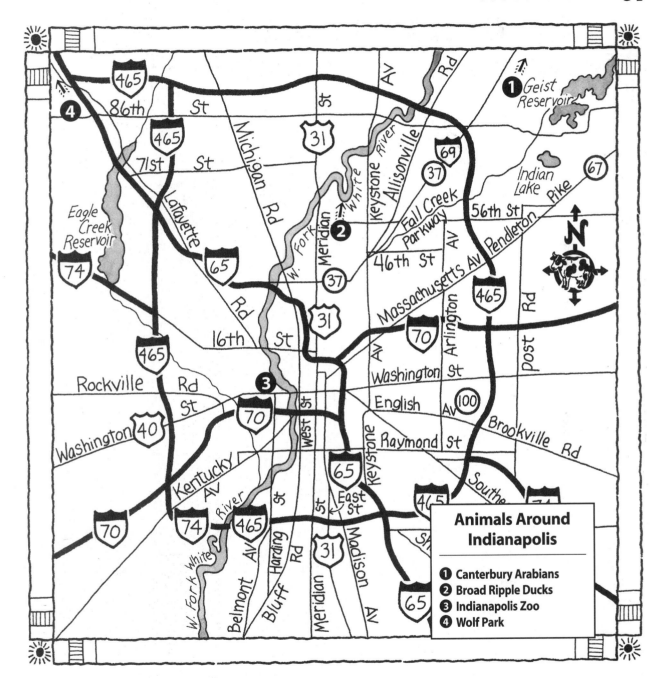

Animals Around Indianapolis

❶ Canterbury Arabians
❷ Broad Ripple Ducks
❸ Indianapolis Zoo
❹ Wolf Park

INDIANAPOLIS ZOO

Have you ever been splashed by a dolphin? Have you ever held a South American cockroach or chased a leopard gecko? At the Indianapolis Zoo, you can do all of these things.

Animals here live in biomes—areas that look like an animal's natural environment. Open exhibits allow you to walk through a scorching desert, hike a humid rainforest trail, or stroll across a grassy African plain. Later, you can cool off by sitting in the front row of the dolphin show.

If you visit during the summer, arrive early in the day when the animals are most active. If you stop by in the evening, go to the Plains biome first. Plains animals have the earliest bedtime of all the zoo animals.

↑ **Guess who has the longest neck in the zoo?**

⇐ **A zoo walrus says hello.**

Animals at the zoo eat 14,000 bales of hay, 8,000 pounds of carrots, 6,500 pounds of oranges, and 72,000 pounds of fish.

HIDDEN MESSAGE

**What is black and white and red all over?
The answer is hidden in the box below. To find it, cross
out all the X's, Y's, K's, F's, G's, W's, J's, Q's, and L's.
The letters remaining spell the answer to this riddle!**

W	A	L	X	S	J	Y	Q	G	J	X	G	J	U	W	F	J
N	L	G	W	L	K	Q	F	B	Y	J	L	X	K	U	Q	L
K	W	R	F	Q	X	L	K	N	K	F	X	Q	Q	X	W	Y
Q	J	K	W	F	L	E	G	X	K	L	G	D	Y	L	L	X
F	L	X	K	Z	F	L	W	L	E	G	F	X	G	W	L	G
Y	L	K	W	X	F	B	W	F	K	X	R	W	F	Q	A	Y

Write the hidden message here:

_____

_____

EAGLE CREEK PARK

Migrating birds recognize Indianapolis as the Crossroads of America just like we do. In March and November, thousands of waterfowl fill the skies and the shores of the bird sanctuary at Eagle Creek Park. Majestic great blue herons, pairs of mallard ducks, and flocks of Canada geese all search for vacancies along the shore.

Bird-watchers can also spot turkey vultures, woodpeckers, and an occasional bald eagle. But the most amusing air traveler could be the Common Goldeneye duck. These small, black ducks dive underwater to feed. After 20 seconds underwater, they burst back to the surface like tiny beach balls.

More information on birds, reptiles, and mammals can be found at the Nature Center. Call the park for hours and prices.

↑ Geese visit the bird sanctuary.

Ms. Kitty is one of the residents at the Nature Center. This red-tailed hawk broke her wing when she was struck by a car. Unable to fly, Ms. Kitty is fed and nurtured by the park's rangers.

BIRD WORD SEARCH

Hidden in this word search are twelve "bird words." Search for words vertically, horizontally, and diagonally. Can you find all 12 words? The first word has been found for you.

Word Box		
beak	hummingbird	seagull
bluejay	nest	tree
cardinal	owl	wing
eggs	robin	wren

```
K O B A Q K M E W O P M E G G S H
W P L E R D Q R Y M H E B T O N H
I Y U Y S U O I N N P T S P A T F
N T E S H U M M I N G B I R D U D
G A J F G M N H D V C E N O J D N
D C A R D I N A L N N O K B S E Y
E D Y Z G X N N C U I U Y I V W R
O B N Q P T I N M K C M N Q N W
R W E G T R R H K F A M W Z C E T
U I L E I E U R N E Y D R V I S B
R O T B L E E T B U L I E Y N T
S E A G U L L Y F O C O N K E
```

BROAD RIPPLE'S BIRDS

It has been said that birds of a feather flock together. In Indianapolis, one of the larger flocks can be found in the village of Broad Ripple. There are so many birds here that duck crossing signs have been put up along the village's main streets.

Ducks and geese spend much of their time wading in the canal or crossing streets to eat the green grass from neighborhood yards. Along with grass, these ducks like to eat bread, crackers, cheese balls, and many other snacks.

For the most fun, throw some bread into the canal near the flock. Then watch as these waterfowl go into a feeding frenzy. Just try to bring enough for everyone!

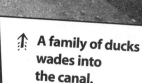

A family of ducks wades into the canal.

Not all geese are friendly. Some will hiss, nip, pinch, or chase you. Sometimes it's best to keep your distance from these feisty fowl.

DUCK, DUCK, GOOSE?

**The pictures above should tell a story, but they're all mixed up!
Can you put them in the correct order by filling in the number box
in the bottom left-hand corner of each picture?**

WOLF PARK

At Wolf Park in Battle Ground, Indiana, you can hold a wolf pup, stand face to face with an adult wolf, and learn to howl. The owners created this park so you can get to know wolves. They're on the endangered species list because as cities grow, wolves lose places to hunt and live.

Scientists are trying to help the wolves find safe places to live—places like national parks or this park. They also want to educate people about wolves. By visiting the park, you will learn that wolves hunt in packs. They are shy and afraid of people. The leader of the pack is the alpha wolf, and the pack communicates with howls, whines, and body language.

When a wolf howls, it's saying, "Here I am. Where are you?" So let out a howl and let the wolves know how you are doing.

There are only 52,000 wolves left in North America.

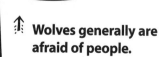
↥ **Wolves generally are afraid of people.**

HOWLING HOOSIER

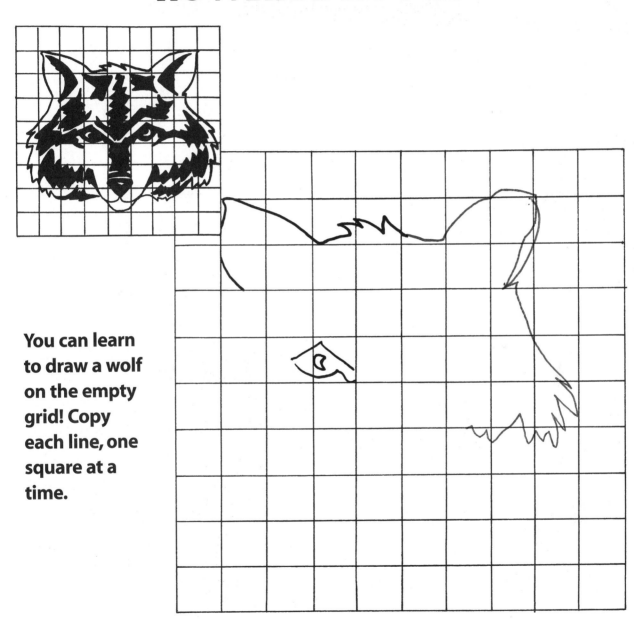

You can learn to draw a wolf on the empty grid! Copy each line, one square at a time.

FARM TOURS

Have you ever slopped a pig? De-tassled a stalk of corn? Milked a cow? By visiting a farm, you'll find that tending crops, feeding animals, and maintaining a farm is interesting and difficult work. That's why many farmers open up their farms and give tours to visitors.

Outside of Indianapolis, there are many miles of farmland. Fields are full of soybeans, corn, hay, dairy and beef cows, pigs, and horses. Here is a list of associations that can help arrange farm tours:

Commissioner of Agriculture (317) 232-8770

The American Dairy Association of Indiana (317) 842-7133

The Indiana Pork Producers Association (317) 872-7500

⬆ **If you visit a farm, you may meet a four-legged friend!**

⬆

A baby cow is called a *calf*.

Indiana is the nation's number one supplier of duck feet. They are considered a delicacy in the Far East.

CROSSWORD FUN

Solve this crossword by figuring out the clues or completing the sentences. If you need help, use the clue box.

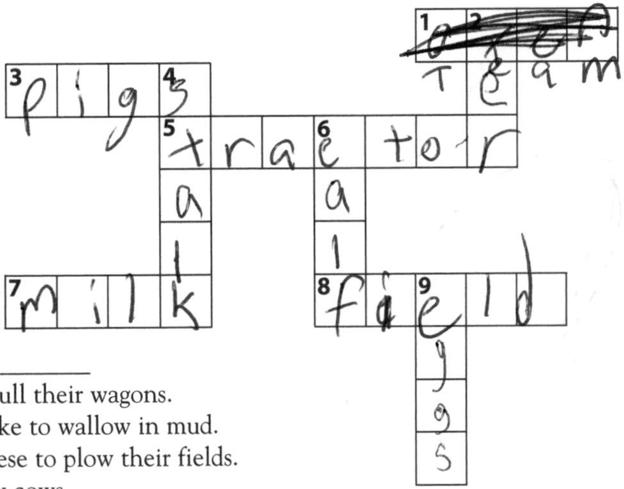

ACROSS

1. Farmers used to use a _______ of horses or oxen to pull their wagons.
3. These farm animals like to wallow in mud.
5. Farmers use one of these to plow their fields.
7. We get this from dairy cows.
8. Where a farmer plants his crops.

DOWN

2. An _______ of corn can't hear a thing.
4. Jack climbed one of these, but his beans were magic.
6. A baby cow, or the back of your leg.
9. You can eat these fried, scrambled, boiled or poached.

Clue Box

eggs	team
stalk	milk
field	ear
tractor	calf
pigs	

CANTERBURY ARABIANS FARM

The one place where you can horse around without upsetting your parents is at Canterbury Arabians Farm. Here, horsing around is their specialty.

Arabians are smart horses and can learn many different tricks. When you stop by for a visit, you can see the horses show off as they exercise. You can also watch as they are bathed, tacked, and groomed. Spring and summer are the best times to see the foals. During the warm months, baby Arabians nip, buck, and nudge one another in the field. They gallop around until they are tired. Then they find a warm spot in the sun and take a nap. All that horsing around can wear you out!

The Indianapolis Colts' mascot, Real Mac, is Canterbury Arabians' star resident.

⇡ Horses love to munch on juicy green grass.

MY TRAVEL JOURNAL
—Animals Around Indianapolis—

I had fun when I visited: _____

I learned about: _____

_____

My favorite animal was: _____

What I enjoyed doing the most was: _____

This is a picture of an animal I saw

 LANDMARKS, SKYSCRAPERS, AND THE ARTS

YOU CAN STAND IN THE SHADOW OF THE ENORMOUS Indiana War Memorial. You can listen to a rousing jazz concert on Madame Walker's stage. Or maybe you would rather spend a quiet moment visiting the gravesite of President Benjamin Harrison or sit at the highest point in the city and admire James Whitcomb Riley's Memorial. If you like music, take in a symphony performance by the Indianapolis Symphony Orchestra, or catch a play at the Indiana Repertory Theatre. Whatever you choose, you'll find all these places are just a short drive or walk away from downtown.

The Indiana Soldiers' and Sailors' Monument

Landmarks, Skyscrapers, and the Arts

1. Arts Garden
2. Crown Hill Cemetery
3. Cenotaph
4. Indiana Repertory Theater
5. Indiana War Memorial
6. Indianapolis Symphony Orchestra
7. Korean War Memorial
8. Madame Walker Building
9. Soldiers' and Sailors' Monument
10. Vietnam War Memorial

MADAME WALKER

At the turn of the century, Madame C.J. Walker developed a successful line of hair-care products. By aggressively selling door-to-door, she was able to establish an office in Pittsburgh, a salon in New York City, and a manufacturing plant in Indianapolis. Her dedication made her the first female black millionaire.

The city of Indianapolis honored her by gracing a building with her name. The wedge-shaped **Walker Building** has long served as a center for African American culture. Famous dancers and jazz and blues legends like Branford Marsalis, Aretha Franklin, and Ella Fitzgerald have performed on the Walker stage.

The Walker Building is at the corner of Indiana Avenue and Martin Luther King Jr.

Madame Walker is one of six women who have been elected to the National Business Hall of Fame.

The Walker Theatre's magnificent stage

MUSIC SCRAMBLE

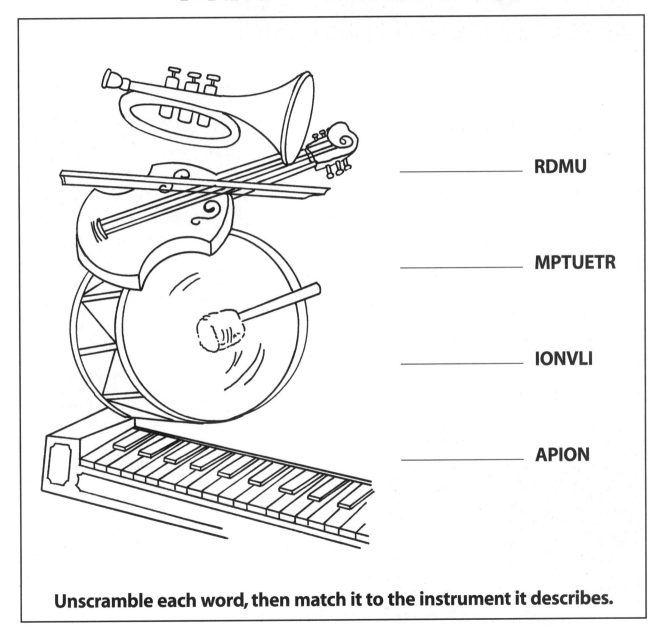

_____ **RDMU**

_____ **MPTUETR**

_____ **IONVLI**

_____ **APION**

Unscramble each word, then match it to the instrument it describes.

INDIANAPOLIS SYMPHONY ORCHESTRA

The Indianapolis Symphony Orchestra (ISO) prides itself on playing over 200 concerts a year. The majority of the concerts are played in the historic **Circle Theater**, which was built in 1916. It was originally the town's grand movie house, but in 1984, the building became the home of the ISO.

The symphony likes to get outdoors, too. During the summer, the ISO moves to the prairie—**Conner Prairie**, that is. "Symphony on the Prairie" is a family-oriented concert series. The audience brings lawn chairs or blankets, listens to Bach and Beethoven, and gazes at the stars.

Another family favorite takes place during December. The "Yuletide Celebration" brings the holidays to life with music, singing, dancing, and giant puppets.

The ISO is one of only 18 symphony orchestras in the country that plays year-round.

↥ Symphony musicians practice for hours to perfect their skills.

SYMPHONY SEARCH

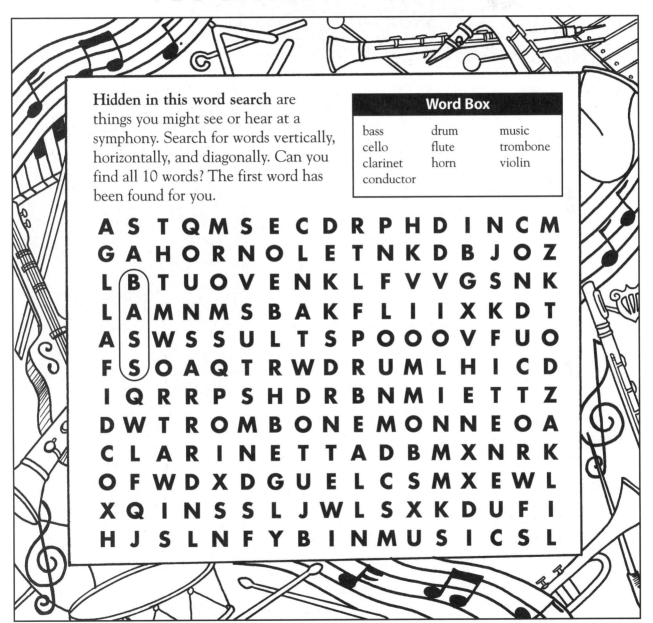

Hidden in this word search are things you might see or hear at a symphony. Search for words vertically, horizontally, and diagonally. Can you find all 10 words? The first word has been found for you.

Word Box		
bass	drum	music
cello	flute	trombone
clarinet	horn	violin
conductor		

```
A S T Q M S E C D R P H D I N C M
G A H O R N O L E T N K D B J O Z
L B T U O V E N K L F V V G S N K
L A M N M S B A K F L I I X K D T
A S W S S U L T S P O O O V F U O
F S O A Q T R W D R U M L H I C D
I Q R R P S H D R B N M I E T T Z
D W T R O M B O N E M O N N E O A
C L A R I N E T T A D B M X N R K
O F W D X D G U E L C S M X E W L
X Q I N S S L J W L S X K D U F I
H J S L N F Y B I N M U S I C S L
```

CROWN HILL CEMETERY

What do cemeteries remind you of? In the movies, graveyards are scary places that are full of zombies, skeletons, and goblins. In reality, they are peaceful resting places brimming with history.

Crown Hill Cemetery is named for its hilltop—the highest point in Indianapolis. This site offers a great view of the entire city. James Whitcomb Riley, the Hoosier Poet, is buried in the cemetery's most scenic spot. When visiting Riley's grave, it's a tradition to leave a penny. Originally, money was left to pay for his elaborate grave site. Today the money is donated to Riley Children's Hospital.

Other famous Hoosiers such as former president Benjamin Harrison, gangster John Dillinger, writer Booth Tarkington, and inventor Richard Gatling (of the Gatling Gun) are all buried here.

⇧ **This is the cemetery as seen from Riley's Gravesite.**

Crown Hill is the fourth largest cemetery in the nation.

CROWN HILL'S CROWN

**Tombstones, tombstones, everywhere! Draw a line connecting
the two tombstones that are alike.**

INDIANA REPERTORY THEATRE

This theater hosts more than 300 plays a year between the months of October and May. So there is a good chance you can see a live performance while you are here. The theater has two different stages: the main stage and the upper stage.

The main stage is reserved for classic and contemporary plays like *A Christmas Carol* and *All My Sons*, while the upper stage hosts many family plays like *Huckleberry Finn* and *Rosa Parks and the Montgomery Bus Boycott*.

The building itself is worthy of a standing ovation. When you are standing in the lobby, you feel like you are in another country. That's because the architects designed it to look like a building in Spain.

In the last 25 years, more than 1,200 actors have performed 4,700 main stage productions in front of 2.5 million people at this theater.

⬆ Actors perform Shakespeare's *Romeo and Juliet* at the Rep.

⬅ The cast of *A Christmas Carol*

HIDE AND SEEK!

Draw circles around all 15 hidden objects in this picture.
When you're done, color in the scene. Look for: a bone, cup,
beach ball, spool of thread, bird, tire, heart, mushroom, book,
sucker, crayon, doorknob, pencil, carrot, and umbrella.

THE ARTS GARDEN

The Arts Garden at Circle Centre Mall is completely surrounded by glass and straddles a downtown intersection, Washington Street at Illinois. The mall owners use this area to bring a wide variety of art to the thousands of shoppers. Everything from jazz, opera, poetry, and rap has been performed on this catwalk stage.

A handful of Saturdays throughout the year are reserved especially for you. Kids will be entertained by storytellers, performers, and other children's artists. Many of these shows are free, but if you don't clap for them, they make you wash every window by hand!

Frank Sinatra made his singing debut in Indianapolis on February 2, 1940.

Distinctive glass windows make the Arts Garden easy to spot.

THE JUGGLING SHOW

Without telling anyone what you're doing, ask for a word to fill in each blank. For example, "Give me an action word." When all the blanks are filled in, read the story out loud. One of the blanks has been filled in for you.

Dax and his friend, _____, were _____ing three
                        name   action word

jugglers as they performed in The Arts Garden. The jugglers joked with

the audience as they tossed _____ __**bells**__ high into the air.
                            describing word   things

"They make it look so easy," Dax said. When the show was over everyone

clapped and _____ ed. As the crowd left the jugglers began to
              sound

_____ their equipment. "Excuse me," said Dax to the jugglers, "but
action word

could you show me how to juggle?"

One of the jugglers smiled and scooped up _____ tiny beanbags.
                                             number

"It's easy," he said, "all you have to do is toss and _____ . Here, you
                                                        action word

try it." He handed Dax the beanbags. "Just don't toss them too hard," he

said, "or you might _____ the windows!"
                      action word

DOWNTOWN MONUMENTS

Indianapolis has many war memorials for the many Indiana residents who fought and died in battle. Since the monuments are all downtown, you can plan a walking tour to see each of them.

Start at the center of town, at the **Indiana Soldiers' and Sailors' Monument**. Built to honor the Civil and Spanish-American War, **Monument Circle** is capped with a bronze statue nicknamed Miss Indiana. Moving north on Meridian street, you'll come to the **Indiana World War Memorial**. This huge, limestone structure holds busts of many famous generals and other war relics.

⬆ **Monument Circle**

The tour finishes at the **Vietnam War and Korean War Memorials** and the **Cenotaph** memorial. Actual letters from soldiers who didn't return from the battlefield are chiseled on the sides of the limestone.

At Christmas, lights are strung from Monument Circle. When the lights come on, the monument becomes a giant Christmas tree.

⬅ **War Memorial Plaza**

MY TRAVEL JOURNAL
—Landmarks, Skyscrapers, and the Arts—

I had fun when I visited: _____

I learned about: _____

My favorite building was: _____

What I enjoyed doing the most was: _____

This is a picture of a building I saw

GOOD SPORTS

WHEN A TOWN IS NICKNAMED "THE AMATEUR SPORTS Capital of the World," you know it is going to have plenty of sports activities to choose from. You can ice skate at Pan Am Plaza or ride bikes at Major Taylor Velodrome. You can in-line skate along the Monon Trail, jog around Eagle Creek Park, or swim at one of the many city pools. Once you've worn yourself out, rest in the stands and cheer for one of Indy's professional sports teams. Your parents can take you out to the ball game—an Indiana Indians game, that is. Sports fans will never be bored in Indianapolis!

⬆ **Cycling is a popular sport in Indianapolis.**

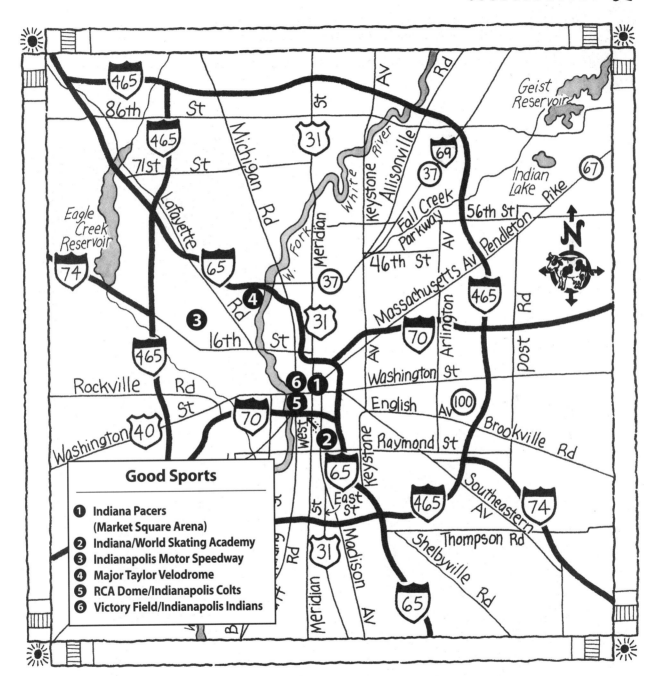

Good Sports

1. **Indiana Pacers**
   (Market Square Arena)
2. **Indiana/World Skating Academy**
3. **Indianapolis Motor Speedway**
4. **Major Taylor Velodrome**
5. **RCA Dome/Indianapolis Colts**
6. **Victory Field/Indianapolis Indians**

THE RCA DOME

The RCA Dome is actually a giant, cloth-covered bubble. Hot air and fans keep the dome from deflating. When you walk through an exit, you can feel yourself getting sucked out the door, so hold on to your hat!

The **Indianapolis Colts** football team calls this bubble house their home. With the exception of game days and major holidays, you can check out their home field. Daily tours will allow you on the field, into the VIP suites, and into the locker rooms.

If you'd rather exercise than tour, stop by the upper level of the Dome. From December through March, it's transformed into **The RollerDome**. You can race around the smooth concourse on in-line skates. The hours and dates vary, so make sure to call ahead.

⇡ **You and your family can tour the RCA Dome.**

⇡ **The RCA Dome's bubble roof is a unique part of the Indianapolis skyline.**

The RCA Dome's roof stretches over eight acres and weighs over 257 tons.

HOME SWEET DOME

These skaters at the RCA dome are each missing an important piece of safety gear. Trace the lines to connect each piece of equipment or clothing to its proper skater.

INDIANAPOLIS INDIANS

The Indians are the minor-league team for the Cincinnati Reds. That means that you can watch some future big-leaguers without having to drive all the way to Ohio. The Indians have one of the best stadiums in the minor leagues. The newly built **Victory Field** looks like a major-league diamond—it's just smaller. Fans are closer to the action and closer to the players.

The Indians love their fans. Many times they will sign autographs before and after games. If you're lucky, they will even slide a bat over the roof of their dugout to you.

Batter up! An aerial view of Victory Field

Baseball players love nicknames. Center fielder Steve Gibralter is nicknamed Rock, as in Rock of Gibralter.

PLAY BALL!

These baseball players are in an action-packed game.
Color the scene.

MAJOR TAYLOR VELODROME

The Major Taylor Velodrome was named after Marshall "Major" Taylor. Born in Indianapolis in 1878, Major went on to win many local, national, and international bicycle races. The highlight of his career was in 1899 when he became the first black World Champion cyclist.

The velodrome has never held a world championship, but many national championships have been held here. In fact, members of the Olympic team trained in Indianapolis to prepare for the Atlanta games. During the summer, they trained in the morning and raced on Friday nights. The track is not reserved for elite cyclists, though. You can pay admission, rent a bike and a helmet, and take a spin on the velodrome's banked turns.

Major earned his nickname when he was a child. To promote a bike shop, he performed bicycle stunts while wearing a military uniform.

⬆ **Racing around the track at the Velodrome**

CROSSWORD FUN

There are lots of ways to have fun bicycling. Solve this crossword by figuring out the clues or completing the sentences. If you need help, use the clue box.

ACROSS

2) Marshall Taylor was the first black World _____ cyclist.
5) Taylor liked to do these on his bike.
6) A bike with three wheels is called this.
7) You need to oil this part of your bike occasionally.
8) Smart cyclists always wear one of these.

DOWN

1) Marshall Taylor got this nickname because he wore a uniform when he did stunts.
3) You can ride on special bike paths in a _____.
4) Many _____ championships have been held at the Velodrome.

Clue Box

Champion	chain
park	Major
national	trike
helmet	stunts

INDIANA/WORLD SKATING ACADEMY

Some days you can admire graceful figure skaters as they glide across the ice at the Indiana/World Skating Academy and Research Center. Other days you'll grimace as burly hockey players slam their opponents into the boards.

If you would rather play than watch, you can skate on one of the Academy's two rinks that are open to the public. If you don't have your own skates, you can rent a pair. As you skate around the rink, you can dream of being the next Michelle Kwan or Dan Jansen. Just watch out for that Zamboni machine!

Wayne Gretzky made his professional hockey debut with the Indianapolis Racers, now known as the Indianapolis Ice.

⇛ **Family fun on the public ice rinks**

SLAP SHOTS AND FIGURE EIGHTS

Without telling anyone what you're doing, ask for a word to fill in each blank. For example, "Give me an action word." When all the blanks are filled in, read the story out loud. One of the blanks has been filled in for you.

Jake and Alex got to the ice rink early. They wanted to see their favorite

_____ practicing before the game that afternoon. "_____ ,
    things   Exclamation

Jake!" shouted Alex. "One of the goalies left their gear and hockey stick.

Jake looked around, but the rink was _____ . He slipped on the
                                         describing word

jersey and face mask, picked up the hockey stick and _____ ed
                                          action word

onto the ice. "Look, I'm a __banana__ " he laughed. Suddenly the players
                                thing

came _____ ing onto the ice. Jake leaped over the wall and into the
         action word

_____ just as _____ forwards crashed into the wall.
   things   number

"Hey," one of them growled, "what kind of goalie are you?" "He's no

goalie," laughed Alex, "he's just a little _____ !"
                                                thing

INDIANAPOLIS MOTOR SPEEDWAY

In years past, balloons, planes, motorcycles, bicycles, and runners have all raced around the Indianapolis Motor Speedway. But on Memorial Day weekend, the track is reserved for the Indianapolis 500. The 33 Indy cars race 500 miles around a 2½-mile oval and have to make 800 left turns to complete the race. What's the biggest mistake a driver can make? Turning right!

Indy car drivers Rick Mears, Mario Andretti, A.J. Foyt, and Al Unser Jr. have all won the Indianapolis 500. Recently, stock car drivers have begun racing on the Indy car oval, too. The Brickyard 400, an annual stock car race, is now held at the Motor Speedway. It doesn't matter what kind of car a driver is racing, his goal is the same—to win the checkered flag.

⬆ **Thirty-three racers compete every year in the Indy 500.**

What did you say? Stock cars are so loud, many of the fans wear earplugs during the race.

INDY CARS AND STOCK CARS

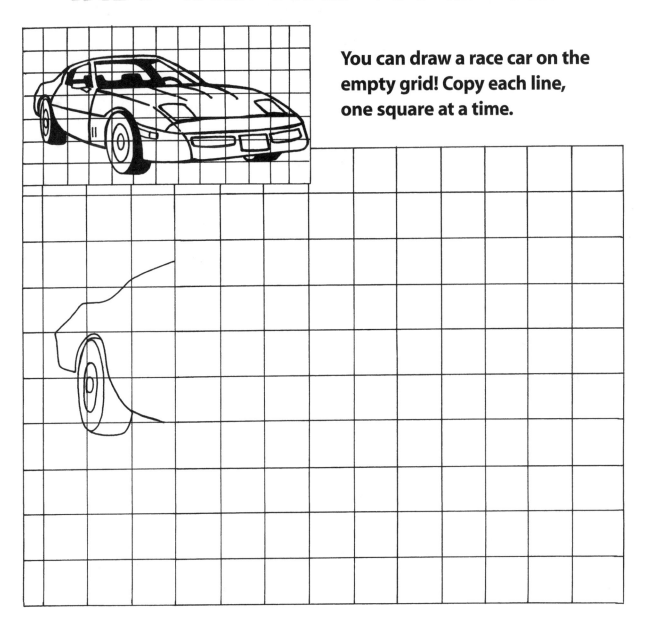

You can draw a race car on the empty grid! Copy each line, one square at a time.

THE INDIANAPOLIS COLTS

⇑
Colts fans pack the RCA Dome.

Question: Do you know what's as loud as a stock car race? Answer: The crowd at the RCA Dome when Marshall Faulk scores a touchdown for the Colts. The fans scream so loudly that many of them are hoarse by the end of the game.

The Colts are a tough team to beat, especially at home. The loud crowd gives the team a real boost. Sometimes they yell, "Goose!" They're not yelling because there's a flock of geese in the dome, they're cheering for Tony Siragusa (Sar-a-GOOS-a), defensive lineman and top quarterback sacker. Whenever he sacks a quarterback or stops a running back for a loss, Tony flaps his arms like a big 300-pound goose.

Tony Siragusa was a state-champion wrestler in high school with a record of 97-1. Would you like to wrestle someone who weighs 320 pounds and once kept a boa constrictor and a tarantula as pets?

DECORATE THE HELMET

Decorate this helmet with
your favorite team logo,
or make a logo of your own.

INDIANA PACERS

Whenever Reggie Miller or another Indiana Pacer hits a 3-point shot, the announcer and the crowd yells, "Boom, baby!" When Reggie isn't sinking shots from the outside, Rik Smits, the Dunking Dutchman, is throwing down a slam dunk. Originally from Denmark, Smits stands over seven feet tall and has scored against players like Shaquille O'Neal and Patrick Ewing.

One of the best dunkers for the Pacers doesn't even play on the team. Boomer, the team's mascot, performs his high-flying, tumbling routine during half time. But unlike Rik Smits, Boomer needs a trampoline to reach the rim.

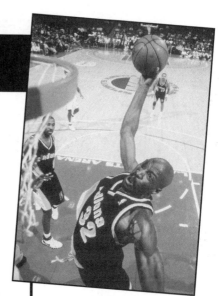

⬆ **Dale Davis slams one home.**

 Reggie Miller goes for a free throw.

While growing up, Reggie Miller's goal was to beat his toughest oponent, his sister. This wasn't just any sister, this was Cheryl Miller—Olympic and college basketball superstar. One night Reggie bragged that he scored 39 points in a game. Cheryl also had a game that night—she scored 105 points!

MY TRAVEL JOURNAL
—Good Sports—

I had fun when I visited:

_____

I learned about: _____

My favorite sport is: _____

I like it because: _____

What I enjoyed doing the most was: _____

This is a picture of something I saw

6 MUSEUMS AND MORE

MUSEUMS DON'T HAVE TO BE STUFFY OLD PLACES WITH boring exhibits and curators telling you not to touch the relics. The Children's Museum of Indianapolis has exhibits you can actually touch, climb in, or fiddle with. At Conner Prairie, the Prairietown residents make you feel as if you've traveled back in time. For a tour of the Old West, visit the Eiteljorg Museum and see Native American and Western art. If traveling by horseback isn't fast enough for you, speed over to the Indianapolis Motor Speedway Hall of Fame Museum. Even the fine art in Indianapolis (by Indiana artists and by artists named Indiana!) can be exciting.

↑ A Western Festival is held each year at the Eiteljorg Museum.

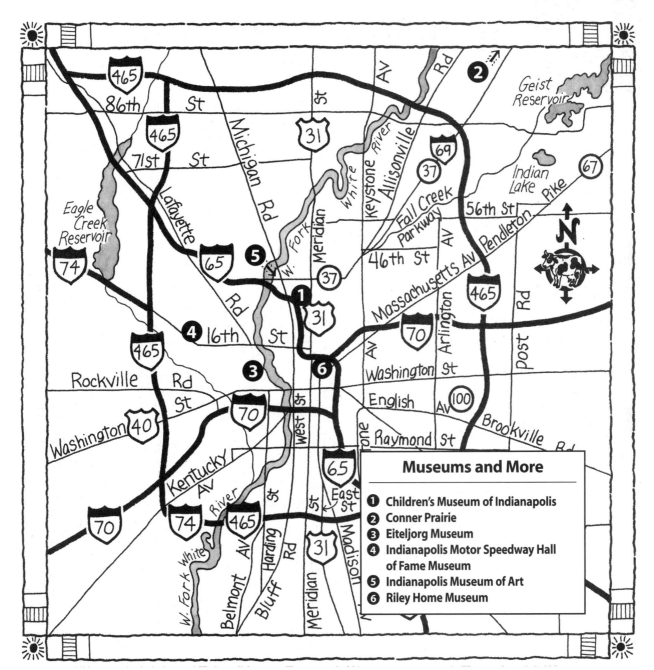

Museums and More

1. Children's Museum of Indianapolis
2. Conner Prairie
3. Eiteljorg Museum
4. Indianapolis Motor Speedway Hall of Fame Museum
5. Indianapolis Museum of Art
6. Riley Home Museum

THE CHILDREN'S MUSEUM

Have you ever visited a place that is covered with "Don't Touch" signs? Well, at the Children's Museum of Indianapolis, their signs read "Please Touch."

Five floors of hands-on exhibits can take a whole day to explore. You can keep time with the world's largest water clock, take a ride on the old-fashioned carousel, sit in a submarine, or explore a mummy's tomb. At the **IWERKS CineDome Theater**, you might find yourself in the middle of the African Serengeti, the ocean, or in an active volcano. The movie screen surrounds you and makes you feel like you are really there.

There is so much to see and touch, the museum is nicknamed the Do-seum.

⬆ **The Children's Museum has an unusual doorman. Rex is a life-sized *Tyrannosaurus rex* that also serves as the museum's mascot.**

CONNECT THE DOTS

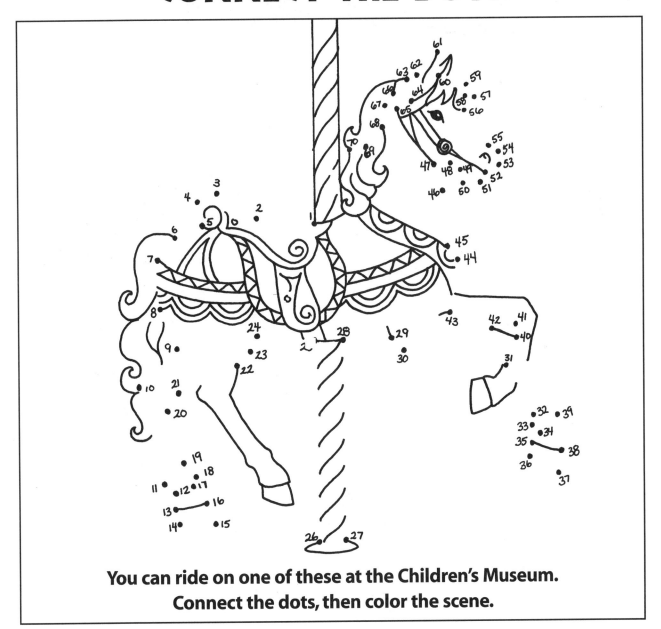

You can ride on one of these at the Children's Museum.
Connect the dots, then color the scene.

THE MUSEUM OF ART

The Indianapolis Museum of Art is as much a park as it is a museum. The grounds of the museum are filled with beautiful trees, shrubs, flowers, gazebos, benches, and sculptures. The *Love* sculpture is one of the largest and easiest to spot. It was created by an artist with a memorable name—Robert Indiana.

Inside the museum you'll find three separate pavilions. Each hosts a portion of the museum's permanent collection. There are many displays by Indiana artists as well as paintings by Rembrandt, the famous Dutch painter.

During the summer, the museum hosts jazz concerts and shows classic movies on the terrace that faces the canal.

⬆ **The Indianapolis Museum of Art is the country's seventh-largest museum.**

⬆ **Robert Indiana's sculpture, *Love***

HIDE AND SEEK

Draw circles around all 15 hidden objects in this picture. When you're done, color in the scene. Look for: a candle, boot, face, baseball, spool, scissors, pencil, bell, cup, painting, heart, sucker, butterfly, key, and ice cream cone.

RILEY HOME MUSEUM

"Such a dear little street it is nestled away
From the noise of the city and the heat of the day."

James Whitcomb Riley wrote this poem to describe Lockerbie Street—the street where he spent the last 23 years of his life. Today, the old Victorian house where he stayed serves as the Riley Home Museum. The furnishings and decorations are just as Riley left them at his death on July 22, 1916. In fact, in an upstairs desk, are his papers, his pen, personal items, and the last poem that he wrote.

Along with poetry, Riley liked to illustrate and play the guitar. His six-string can be found leaning against a mirror in the entrance hall. He also loved his dog Lockerbie so much that there is a painting of the poodle in the house.

⬆ **The Hoosier Poet lived in this house until 1916.**

James Whitcomb Riley has had 1,044 of his poems published.

DOGGIE DELIGHTS

Each of these dogs has something in common with the two others in the same row. For example, the top row of dogs all have bows on their heads. Draw a line through each row and describe what the dogs in that row have in common. Don't forget the diagonals!

MOTOR SPEEDWAY HALL OF FAME

The Indianapolis Motor Speedway Hall of Fame Museum is like the race it's named after. Both the race and the museum have a lineup of 33 cars. The difference is that the museum's cars are all winners.

The museum often has to rotate its displays. That's because so many Indy 500 race winners have donated goggles, helmets, race suits, shoes, and other racing memorabilia. In the **Hulman Theater**, you can watch a film that documents the history of the 500.

Tour buses offer rides around the track itself. They don't travel as fast as the race cars, though. The tour guides would have a hard time pointing out the sights while passing them at 230 miles per hour!

Four of the museum's winning cars were driven by A.J. Foyt who won the race in 1961, 1964, 1967, and 1977.

⇑ **Winning cars, along with photos and trophies, are on display.**

⇑ **The museum is located at the Motor Speedway.**

COMING THROUGH!

Can you help this race car get to the finish line?
Watch out for obstacles!

EITELJORG MUSEUM

Harrison Eiteljorg once said, "I went on a trip west looking for coal, and in the process fell in love with the West and Western art." So, upon his return to Indianapolis, he opened the Eiteljorg Museum.

Watch your step as you walk into the lobby of this American Indian and Western art museum. A mural painting of the Grand Canyon looks so real, it makes you feel like you could fall right over the edge. Native American artifacts, paintings, pottery, basketry, and clothing are all part of the permanent and traveling exhibits. Other Western artists have their paintings and sculptures on display both inside and outside the museum.

The exhibits, the architecture, and even the trees around the museum will make you feel like you have traveled to the Old West.

The Wild West comes to life at the Eiteljorg.

The Eiteljorg is one of two museums east of the Mississippi that displays both Native American art and Western paintings and bronzes.

WHICH IS THE SAME?

Native American pottery comes in many sizes and with many different patterns. Draw a line connecting the two pots that are the same.

CONNER PRAIRIE

If you ask one of the Prairietown actors at Conner Prairie who the president is, you might get a surprise. They'll tell you that it's Andrew Jackson. They'll also tell you that they've never heard of Bill Clinton and have never seen a car, or a computer for that matter.

That's because these actors are living in the year 1836. By stepping back in time, you can learn about life in an early Indiana settlement. You can watch a blacksmith make a horseshoe, learn how to spin yarn, or even help unload the firewood wagon as it makes its rounds.

In the **Weaver Gallery**, there is a modern computer game where you can load a wagon or learn about a canal lock. Just don't ask the folks at Prairietown to help you use it.

The Prairietown shopkeepers love to talk about 1836 politics. Ask a shopkeeper what he thinks of William Henry Harrison's chances to become president.

⇐
Women dressed like this in the 1830s.

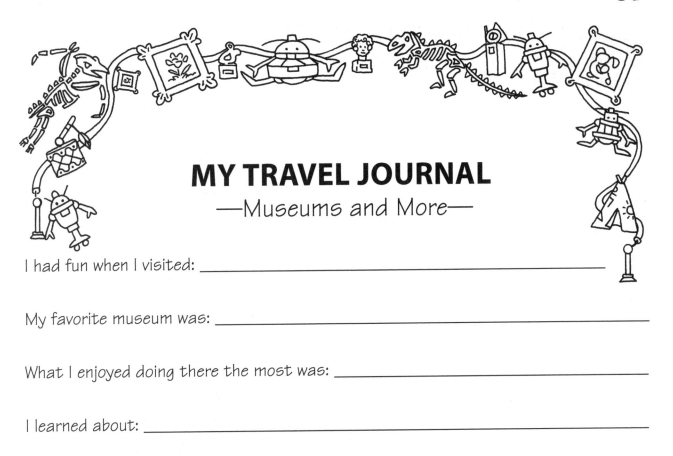

MY TRAVEL JOURNAL
—Museums and More—

I had fun when I visited: _____

My favorite museum was: _____

What I enjoyed doing there the most was: _____

I learned about: _____

This is a picture of a painting or sculpture I saw

THAT'S ENTERTAINMENT

HAVE YOU EVER HEARD SOMEONE SAY, "shop 'til you drop," "swim like a fish," "see the stars," or "catch a flick"? In Indianapolis these aren't just sayings, they're real, fun things to do during your visit. At Circle Centre Mall, there are enough shops, eateries, video games, and movie selections to fill up an entire day. If you'd rather splash than shop, make a trip over to Indy Island. This indoor water park is open year-round and has some awesome water slides. Moving from aquatics to astronomy, you can peer at some planets, comets, or the moon at the Holcomb Observatory. After peering into the galaxy, you can try your luck at duckpin bowling. It's like regular bowling except the balls and pins are smaller—*quack!*

⇡ **The aquatic center at Garfield Park**

465

86th St

465

71st St

Michigan Rd

31 St

AV

Rd

Geist Reservoir

White River

Keystone River

Allisonville

69

37

Indian Lake

Pike

67

Eagle Creek Reservoir

Lafayette

65

W. Fork

Meridian

4 37

46th St

Fall Creek Parkway

AV

56th St

Massachusetts Av

Pendleton

465

74

Rd

16th St

31

AV

70

Arlington St

Post Rd

N

Rockville Rd

5 2

St

Washington St

465

70

West St

English

AV 100

Brookville Rd

Washington 40

65

1

Keystone

Raymond St

6

entucky

East St

31

Madison AV

3 465

Southeastern AV

74

Thompson Rd

Shelbyville Rd

Meridian St

65

That's Entertainment

1 **Action Bowl**
2 **Circle Centre Mall**
3 **Greatimes**
4 **Holcomb Observatory**
5 **IMAX 3D Movie Theater**
6 **Indy Island**

DOWNTOWN SHOPPING

Shopping at the **Circle Centre Mall** is like shopping in Chicago or New York City—without all of the traffic or as many people. It has toy stores, clothing shops, gift boutiques, Disney and Warner Bros. stores, a theater, and restaurants. There's also a giant arcade where you can race Indy and stock cars or motorcycles or ski down a mountain. In the Virtual Reality section you can feel like you are flying a hang glider.

During the holidays, you can sit in the Arts Garden and listen to choirs or bands sing and play Christmas music. Instead of calling it a shopping mall, they should call it an eating-playing-dancing-singing-and-watching-a-movie mall.

↟ **If you like to shop, don't miss Circle Centre Mall.**

⇐ **Experience virtual reality in the mall arcade.**

The Circle Centre Mall covers nearly two city blocks.

TOYS GALORE

Can you help this store's owners decorate their shop? Use your pencil or crayons to fill the toy store window with toys.

QUACK! IT'S DUCKPIN BOWLING

↑
Duckpin bowling pins and balls are just the right size—kid-size!

Going duckpin bowling at the Action Bowl in Fountain Square is like traveling back in time. An old-fashioned elevator, complete with an elevator operator, takes you up to the fourth-floor bowling alley. The ball return is over 90 years old, the pool table was built in 1918, and the bar comes from the 1950s. Even the game itself is old-fashioned.

Duckpin bowling was invented in 1900, and not much has changed over the years. The pins and balls are smaller than those used in normal bowling. You also get three chances to knock down all of the pins.

←
Historic Fountain Square

The two Action Bowl locations in Indianapolis are the only duckpin bowling alleys in the Midwest.

DUCKPIN BOWLING

Hidden in this word search are some things you might see or do at a bowling alley. Search for words vertically, horizontally, and diagonally. Can you find all 10 words? The first word has been found for you.

Word Box

alley	pins	spare
ball	return	strike
gutter	score	
lanes	shoes	

```
C U G E W L S S G N X S T R I K E
H A H B R D Q S Y L H E B A E N H
N Y N A S G P I N N A T S A X T F
T T A L L E Y E G T K N G D R P D
R R T L G K R R D V U E E O E I N
X R U V M A M N G N S S G S G N Y
E E S S P U N N H U G C Y O B S R
S T A S P E I N D K C O M H D D W
I U R C U K G U T T E R G F J Q T
U R S E I S U R N N Y E N L M U B
R N T B L S R T U U L X B Y N F S
D Y D N I O F Y H S H O E S E Q R
```

HOLCOMB OBSERVATORY

On cloudless nights at Holcomb Observatory you can peer deep into the galaxy. You can watch a planetarium show, see the clock room with its Geochron world time piece, and take a close-up look at the stars and planets through the largest telescope in Indiana.

Did you know that you could find your way using the stars as a compass? Locate the Big Dipper, the constellation that looks like a big spoon. Draw an imaginary line from the two stars farthest from its handle to the North Star, the brightest star nearby in the sky. Draw another imaginary line straight down from the North Star to the horizon. That point is north, directly behind you is south, to the right is east, and the left is west.

The observatory, at Butler University, is open to the public. Call ahead to get the dates and times of upcoming shows.

⬆ **The observatory's domed roof holds a powerful telescope**

SEE THE STARS

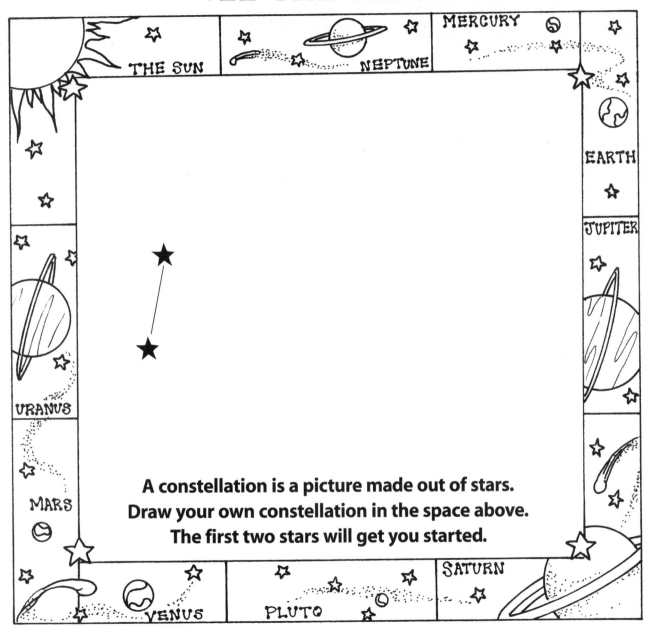

A constellation is a picture made out of stars.
Draw your own constellation in the space above.
The first two stars will get you started.

GREATIMES

If you want to settle for just a good time, you shouldn't go to Greatimes. There is so much to do, you can't help but have fun. You can climb into the bumper boats and slam into your dad. You can strap yourself into a Go-Kart and race against your sister.

⇡ **If you like to play games, you'll love Greatimes.**

If ball sports are more your game, you can practice your putts on the miniature golf course or perfect your swing in the batting cages. There are also games that award you with tickets that can be cashed in for prizes. Remember to bring in your report card—if you have high marks you can get free tickets and video game tokens.

Greatimes has thrown a few birthday parties. Last year, they helped over 5,000 people celebrate their special day.

WHICH IS THE SAME?

Two of the kids and their bumper cars above are twins.
Circle the two that are exactly the same.

INDY ISLAND

Even when it's winter, don't forget to pack your swimsuit. In Indianapolis, most city pools open on Memorial Day and close on Labor Day. But now that Indy Island is open, you can swim year-round. Swimming in this indoor water park is only part of the fun. There is a wading pool, a wave pool, and even a 150-foot spiral water slide. On the pool deck you'll find basketball and volleyball courts.

So when the outdoor pools are frozen solid, you can be splashing, sliding, and swimming until you're all tired out.

⬆ **Are you brave enough to try the spiral slide?**

Gustave Brickner holds the world record for most miles swam in a lifetime— 38,512!

SUPER SLIDERS

**These kids slid down the water slides and left their towels behind.
By tracing each slider back to where he or she started,
can you discover who each towel belongs to?**

IMAX 3D THEATER

Do you like watching movies on the big screen? How about 3D movies on a screen that's ten times bigger than a regular silver screen? If that's the case, you'll love the IMAX 3D movie theater.

When you enter the theater, you'll be given a pair of polarized glasses. The glasses, combined with the 6-story screen, will make it seem like you're in the middle of the action. One movie takes you on a roller coaster ride that has you holding on to your chair and leaning into the turns. Another has you face-to-face with a mountain lion as it jumps right at you. Yet another has you survive a crash-landing on a snowy mountain range. So hold on to your popcorn!

⇑
A giant-sized screen needs a giant-sized theater.

There are only 24 IMAX 3D theaters in the world.

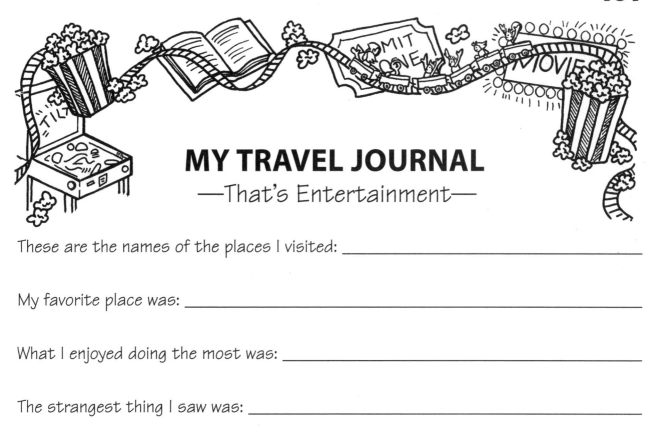

MY TRAVEL JOURNAL
—That's Entertainment—

These are the names of the places I visited: _____

My favorite place was: _____

What I enjoyed doing the most was: _____

The strangest thing I saw was: _____

This is a picture of something I saw ▸

8 LET'S EAT

AROUND THE CIRCLE CITY THERE IS A SAYING: "You can call me anything you'd like; just don't call me late for dinner." With so many great places to eat, you wouldn't want to be late for breakfast or lunch, either.

Whether your favorite food is pizza, spaghetti, tacos, or soups and salads, you'll be able to find a restaurant to satisfy your appetite. In fact, there's one place that has all of those restaurants and more—all under one roof. Other restaurants in town have sections that don't have any roofs at all. So while you're dining, the sun is shining on your face and a warm breeze is blowing through your hair.

When the dinner bell rings, all you have to decide is whether you like country cooking or another country's cooking, eating on a patio or in a trolley car, dining out or carry out, Mexican or Mediterranean, Mmmm. Are you hungry, yet?

⇧ Seafood vendors sell fish at the city market.

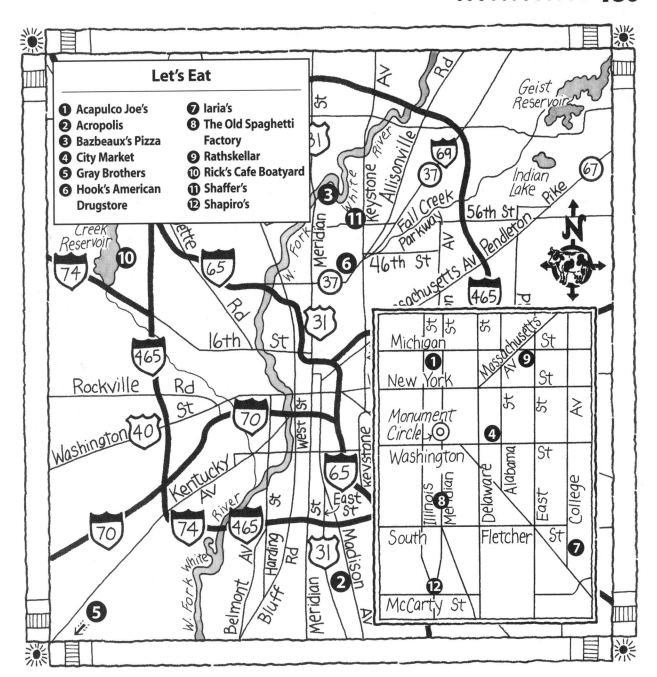

LET'S DO LUNCH

The **City Market** is a lunchtime favorite for locals. You can get a jumbo roast beef sandwich, pizza, Chinese food, ice cream, or cookies. There are also stands that sell fruits, vegetables, or newspapers so you can get some food and reading material to go.

Another midday favorite is **Shapiro's Deli**. This kosher-style deli's specialties are large Reuben and pastrami sandwiches. They also serve a selection of other sandwiches, soups, hot dishes, and incredible desserts.

⇑ **Buy fresh fruits and vegetables at City Market.**

The City Market was constructed in 1832, destroyed by a fire in 1958, and then renovated in 1977.

WHAT'S THE DIFFERENCE?

**These two pictures might look the same, but they are not.
How many differences between the two scenes can you find?
Hint: There are at least 15 differences.**

MEDITERRANEAN AND MEXICAN

Opa! If you crave meaty gyros or sweet baklava, your family should check out **The Acropolis** in Southport. This Greek restaurant offers a Mediterranean menu of unique dinners and desserts. On weekends, a belly dancer, complete with castanets, gets everyone clapping and keeps you entertained.

If spicy tacos, sizzling fajitas, or cheesy *chile con queso* are what you want, **Acapulco Joe's** will take your order. At this downtown Mexican restaurant, you can see pictures of Joe himself, eat salsa from a squirt bottle, and sing "God Bless America" with the entire restaurant. *Ole!*

Feta is a hard, crumbly Greek cheese made from goat's or sheep's milk.

⇛
Acapulco Joe's was the first Mexican restaurant in Indianapolis.

HIDE AND SEEK

**Draw circles around all 15 hidden objects in this picture.
When you're done, color in the scene. Look for: a cherry, horn,
teapot, doughnut, cup, baseball, baseball bat, comb, mouse,
dog head, ruler, golf hole and flag, tie, bell, and bird.**

PASTA AND PIZZA

Iaria's has a menu that's loaded with fettuccini, ravioli, lasagna, garlic bread, and spumoni ice cream. This Italian restaurant has been in Indianapolis since 1933. Although there is a fancier Italian restaurant right next door, many of the locals will still pick Iaria's.

Sure, you could get pizza at an Italian restaurant, but why not go to a place that specializes in pizza? **Bazbeaux's Pizza** in Broad Ripple has more pizza toppings than Dennis Rodman has hair colors. There are 52 different toppings, and a variety of crusts and homemade sauces. It's not difficult to decide to eat there. The difficulty comes in choosing what to eat once you're there.

In Costa Rica, people like to top their pizzas with coconut. In Japan, it's not uncommon to see toppings like eel and squid.

←

Bazbeaux's has so many pizzas, you can order a differrent kind every time you go.

PIZZA, PIZZA

**Find the slice of pizza on the left that matches the pizza on the right.
Then draw a line connecting each slice with its pizza.**

FONDUE AND ICE CREAM SODAS

"Fondue" is French for "to melt."

When the waiters at **Shaffer's** bring out the fondue, they yell, "Hot oil!" That's so others don't step in front of them and get a hot oil bath! Shaffer's specializes in fondue. That means that you get to cook your food at your table. Dip bread into the cheese fondue. Cook chicken, seafood, or beef in the oil fondue. And there is chocolate fondue for dessert.

After cooking with hot oil, it's time to get some cold ice cream. The best ice-cream sodas in Indy are made at **Hook's American Drugstore Museum**. This nineteenth-century drugstore has antique jars full of candy and a marble-topped soda fountain. Each soda is hand-dipped, mixed with chocolate syrup and seltzer, and then topped with whipped cream and a cherry. After you slurp that last sip, they'll wash the glass and let you take it home with you.

⬆ **Enjoy ice cream treats and more at Hook's.**

ICE CREAM

Hidden in this word search are words you might see (or taste) in an ice cream shop. Search for words vertically, horizontally, and diagonally. Can you find all 10 words? The first word has been found for you.

Word Box

chocolate	peppermint	sundae
cone	rocky road	vanilla
fudge	sherbet	
peach	strawberry	

```
K P E P P E R M I N T M Y P D U H
H C H F R D O N Y M H E M A O P H
N H N Q S G C I N D P T S L V E S
T O P O D R K K A V A N I L L A T
R C T T G U Y S S V C E K T X C R
D O U E D D R N U N N O G Y Y H A
E L S V G L O N N G I F Y E J W W
S A X C P C A K D K C U M R A L B
P T X D O Z D O A B W D E R L Q E
U E S T I N Y R E U I G N L O U R
R O T B A K E T E U L E M S N F R
S H E R B E T D F R F S B G K Q Y
```

FACTORY OR FAMILY FOOD

At the **Old Spaghetti Factory** your family can feast on salad, garlic bread, and (of course) spaghetti without spending a lot of money. Not only is it an inexpensive restaurant, but it's also a fun place to eat. They have just about every spaghetti sauce imaginable. You can dine in a trolley car that sits in the middle of the restaurant.

For a more traditional, home-cooked meal, it's hard to beat **Gray Brothers Cafeteria** in Mooresville. It's so good that everyone has to wait in line for the food. Try the pies (pumpkin, apple, and banana cream) and the chicken and noodles. The swiss steak and roast beef are definitely worth the wait. It's so good, you'll swear your grandma is in their kitchen doing all of the cooking.

Spaghetti was invented by the Chinese. It was brought back to Italy by world explorer Marco Polo.

⬅ **You can eat in a trolley car at the Old Spaghetti Factory.**

LOTSA PASTA

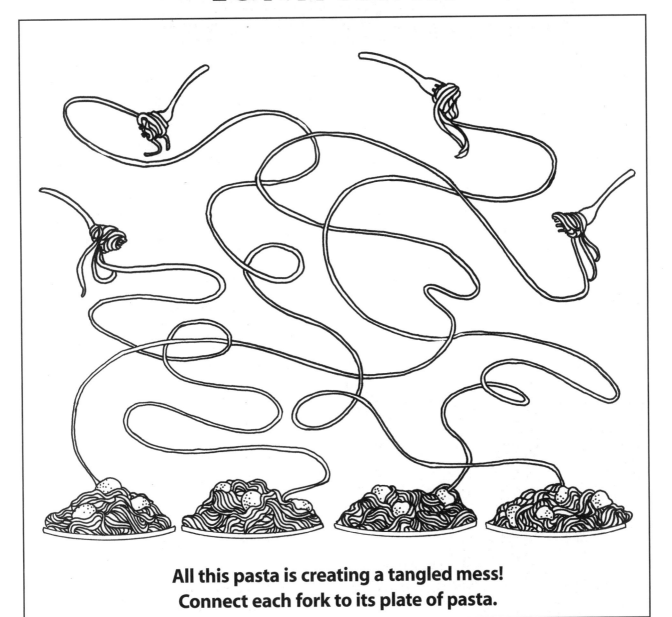

**All this pasta is creating a tangled mess!
Connect each fork to its plate of pasta.**

OTHER FUN SPOTS

The **Rathskeller Restaurant** is called an Old World restaurant. One reason is that the restaurant is housed in a historic German building called the Athenaeum. The dim lighting and the stone walls make you feel like you're eating in a dungeon. But prisoners aren't fed this well. Everything from classic to gourmet German food will have you asking for *mehr* (more).

If it's American food you want, then you can't get much more American than **Rick's Café Boatyard**. The restaurant is across the street from a small airport and sits on the bank of Eagle Creek Reservoir. Guests can fly, boat, or drive up to the door. Call ahead and reserve a table outside and watch the sunset over the reservoir.

When you dine outside, that's called eating alfresco. "Alfresco" is Italian for "in the open air."

⇧ **Boats sail by the window while you dine at Rick's.**

MY TRAVEL JOURNAL
—Let's Eat!—

These are the names of some of the restaurants I ate at:

_____

My favorite restaurant was: _____

The food I enjoyed there the most was: _____

The most unusual food I ate was: _____

Mt least favorite food was: _____

This is a picture of one restaurant I visited

CALENDAR OF INDIANAPOLIS EVENTS

January

Cross-Country Skiing
Eagle Creek Park, (317) 327-7110
If there's enough snow, cross-country skis offer a great way to see the park.

New Year's Day
& Martin Luther King Day
The Indianapolis Children's Museum,
(317) 924-5431
Since school is out on these days, the museum is packed full of people and adventures.

February

Chinese New Year
Indianapolis Association of Chinese American and U.S. People Association, (317) 547-3641

Maple Sugar Program
Conner Prairie, (317) 773-0666
Learn how watery maple tree sap is transformed into pancake syrup.

Black History Month
Madame Walker Urban Center, (317) 236-2099
Films, music, and other activities planned at various locations around the city.

Kidsfest
RCA Dome, (317) 637-4574
This indoor fair has a midway, food, and games.

↥ American Legion Plaza

Boat, Sport, and Travel Show
Indiana State Fairgrounds, (317) 927-7500
Includes boats, campers, fishing gear, and other outdoor equipment.

March

St. Patrick's Day Parade
Indianapolis Athletic Club, March 17,
(317) 634-4331
Downtown parade route provides plenty of shamrocks, leprechauns, blarney, and bands.

April

Arbor Day
Division of Forestry, the last Friday in April,
(317) 232-4105
Free tree seedlings are given to the public.

Book and Author Luncheon
Christamore Aid Society, (317) 842-4356
Four published authors speak and autograph their latest works.

May

Broad Ripple Art Fair
Indianapolis Art League, (317) 255-2464
More than 200 artists display and sell their art in a street fair setting.

Mini-Marathon
Indy Festival Inc., (317) 636-4556
This 13-mile race is the largest mini-marathon in the country.

500 Parade
Indy Festival Inc., (317) 636-4556
The downtown parade route has floats, Indy cars, drivers, marching bands, and more.

The Indianapolis 500
Indianapolis Motor Speedway, Memorial Day Weekend, (317) 481-8500
The famous 500 mile race that takes Indy cars only three hours to finish.

June

Flag Day
American Legion, June 14, (317) 630-1200
Celebrate to remember this date in 1777 when the Continental Congress designated Old Glory as our national emblem.

Midsummer Festival
Cathedral Arts, summer solstice, (317) 637-4574
Bands, food booths, and strolling entertainment mark the longest day of the year.

State Political Conventions
Even-numbered years. Republicans, (317) 635-7561; Democrats, (317) 231-7100
A first-hand view of politics. Check with party headquarters for ticket procedures.

Strawberry Festival
Christ Church Cathedral, (317) 636-4577
The festival is held each year on the Circle. Volunteers serve bowls of fresh strawberry shortcake.

Symphony on the Prairie
Indiana Symphony Orchestra, (317) 639-4300
The Indianapolis orchestra moves to the great outdoors at Conner Prairie.

Talbott Street Art Fair
Indiana Artist-Craftsmen Inc, (317) 257-4687

July

Black Expo
Black Expo Inc, (317) 925-2702
Music, art exhibits, and entertainment that celebrates African American culture.

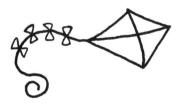

County Fairs

Marion County, southeast side of Indianapolis; Hancock County, Greenfield; Hendricks County, Danville; Hamilton County, Noblesville; Johnson County, Franklin

Check out the 4-H exhibits, horse shows, greased-pig competitions, and melon eating and seed spitting contests.

Fourth of July

Downtown Indianapolis

Fireworks are launched from the Indiana Bank Tower.

Fourth of July

Conner Prairie

Races, tug-o-wars, and dramas mark an old-fashioned Independence Day.

Soap Box Derby

Wilbur Shaw Hill, Bob Snoddy, (317) 738-2812

August

American Indian Council Traditional Pow Wow

Boone County 4-H Grounds, (317) 482-3315

Native Americans from the Midwest gather. You'll see dancing, arts and crafts, traditional clothing, and food.

Amish Country Market

Hamilton County Fairgrounds, (317) 545-1970

Buggy rides, quilts, country cooking, and baking offer a peek into the Amish lifestyle.

⇡ **Swing high, swing low at Holliday Park**

Benjamin Harrison's Birthday

Benjamin Harrison Home, (317) 631-1898

There is a birthday party at the home and a wreath laying at his grave site.

Hoosier Storytelling Festival

Stories Inc., (317) 576-9848

Expert storytellers give demonstrations and workshops.

Indiana Avenue Jazz Festival

Madame Walker Urban Life Center, (317) 236-2088

Local and nationally known jazz musicians play at this free concert.

Brickyard 400

Indianapolis Motor Speedway, (317) 481-8500

Jeff Gordon, Dale Earnhardt, and others roar around the Motor Speedway in this stock car race.

Indiana State Fair

Indiana State Fairgrounds, (317) 923-3431

Great food, games, midway, exhibits, and animal barns mark the summer's last hurrah.

RCA Championships
Indianapolis Tennis Center, (317) 278-2100
Past tournament winners include: Boris Becker,
Pete Sampras, and Andre Agassi.

Oktoberfest
German Park, (317) 888-6940

September

Greek Food Festival
Holy Trinity Greek Orthodox Church,
(317) 283-3816
Flaming cheese, baklava, and honey-dipped
chicken are served while Greek music plays.

Home Tour
Old Northside Inc. House Tour, (317) 631-1898
See historic, restored homes on Indianapolis' north
side.

National Hot Rod Association,
U.S. Nationals
Indianapolis Raceway Park, (317) 291-4090
Funny cars and top fuel dragsters cover the quarter-
mile race strip in less than four seconds.

Penrod Art Fair
Indianapolis Museum of Art, (317) 923-1331
Penrod is one of the largest art fairs in the state.
Music, food, dance, and art for display and purchase
fill the museum's grounds.

Western Festival/Chili and
BBQ State Championship Cookoff
Eiteljorg Museum, (317) 636-9378
Eat tender BBQ and hot, hot chili while looking at
western art and listening to western music.

Brickyard Crossing Championship
Brickyard Crossing Golf Course, (317) 484-6559
Many top professional golfers play in this
tournament.

October

International Festival
Nationalities Council, (317) 849-3105
International cultures put on displays of food,
dancing, and art.

James Whitcomb Riley's Birthday
Riley Festival Committee, (317) 462-4188
Parade and entertainment held in Greenfield,
Riley's birthplace.

**An Indian Market is
held at the Eiteljorg
Museum every
September**

Stonycreek Farm Festival
Stonycreek Farm, (317) 773-3344
There will be hay rides, a haunted barn, petting zoo, and a chance to pick your own pumpkin.

Halloween
The Children's Museum Haunted House, (317) 924-5431

Halloween
Hannah House, (317) 787-8486

Halloween
The Legend of Sleepy Hollow, Conner Prairie, (317) 274-2273

November

The Lighting of the Monument
Indianapolis Downtown Inc., Friday after Thanksgiving, (317) 237-2222
Santa will help light the "world's tallest Christmas tree."

Veteran's Day Parade
Indiana War Memorials, Armistice Day, (317) 232-7615
Celebrates the end of World War I, as well as the sacrifices made by all veterans.

Picture Your Pet with Santa
Humane Society, (317) 872-5650
For a small fee, your pet can pose for a picture with Santa.

December

Yuletide Feast
Trinity Episcopal Church, (317) 923-1346
The feast is set in twelfth/fifteenth century England complete with madrigals, costumed musicians, and traditional plum pudding.

Winterland
Indiana State Fairgrounds, (317) 927-7500
Two million holiday lights create many de-light-ful displays.

Christmas at the Zoo
Indianapolis Zoo, (317) 630-2001
There will be animal sculptures, carriage rides, snowmen, and Santa Claus.

For more listings of events through the year check: the *Indianapolis Star*, Friday and Sunday editions; the *Indianapolis News*, Friday edition; *Nuvo News Weekly*.

RESOURCE GUIDE: WHEN, WHAT, AND HOW MUCH?

Although all of the sites listed in this guide offer programs for children and families, not all programs offered by these places are suitable. Before attending a theater production, have your parents call ahead to check if the program is OK for you to see.

The information in this Resource Guide changes often. Call before you plan your trip for current costs and hours of admission.

If You Get Lost

Do you know what to do if you get lost? Make a plan with your parents about what to do if you lose them. If you are in a store, go to a person working at a cash register. If you are outside, look for a mother with children, and tell her that you are lost.

If there is an emergency and you need the police, fire department, or an ambulance, you can dial 911 from any phone at no charge.

Important numbers

Injury, accident, or emergency 911
Indianapolis Police Department
  (317) 327-3811
Indianapolis Convention and Visitors Association
  (317) 639-4282
Airport Visitors Center (317) 487-7243
Indianapolis Poison Center (317) 929-2323
Indiana State Police (800) 582-8440

Indiana State Police Missing Children
  (800) 831-8953
Weather and Time of Day (317) 635-5959

Transportation

Car Rentals:
  Avis (317) 248-4860
  Budget (317) 248-1100
  Enterprise (317) 848-2200

Circle Express (317) 240-6124
Metro Bus (317) 632-1900
Gray Line of Indianapolis (tour)
  (317) 587-1798

Taxis:
  Yellow Cab (317) 487-7777
  Hoosier Cab (317) 243-8800
  Metro Taxi (317) 634-1111

What They Cost and When They're Open

Acapulco Joe's Mexican Foods, 365 North Illinois Street, Indianapolis. Breakfast on Monday through Friday from 7 a.m. to 10:30 a.m., Lunch from 10:30 a.m. to 4 p.m., Dinner from 4 p.m. to 9 p.m. and Saturday from 4 p.m. to 10 p.m. (317) 637-5160

Acropolis Restaurant, 1625 East Southport Road, Southport, 46227. Monday through Friday from 11 a.m. to 10 p.m., Friday and Saturday from 11 a.m. to 11 p.m. (belly dancer present at dinner), Sunday from 2 p.m. to 9 p.m. (317) 787-8883

Action Bowl, 1105 East Prospect Street, Indianapolis, 46203. Monday through Thursday from 11 a.m. to 10 p.m., Friday from 11 a.m. to 1 a.m., Saturday from noon to 1 a.m., closed Sunday. Cost $16 per hour, $1.50 for shoes. (317) 686-6006

Adrian Orchard, 500 West Epler Avenue, Indianapolis, 46227. Call after Labor Day to schedule a tour, minimum of 20 people. Open from June to January (longer if necessary), Monday through Saturday from 9 a.m. to 7 p.m., Sunday from 10 a.m. to 6 p.m. Cost $1.50 per person. (317) 784-0550

American Dairy Association of Indiana, 9360 Castlegate Drive, Indianapolis, 46256. (317) 842-7955

Bazbeaux's Pizza, 832 East Westfield Boulevard, Broad Ripple, 46220. Open Monday through Thursday from 11 a.m. to 2:30 p.m. with dinner from 4:30 p.m. to 10 p.m., Friday and Saturday from 11 a.m. to 2:30 p.m. with dinner from 4:30 p.m. to midnight, Sunday from noon to 10 p.m. (317) 255-5711

Benjamin Harrison Home, 1230 North Delaware Street Indianapolis, 46202. Monday through Saturday from 10 a.m. to 3:30 p.m., Sunday from 12:30 p.m. to 3:30 p.m. Admission is $3 for adults, $1 for children, and $2.50 for seniors. (317) 631-1898

Canterbury Arabians, 12131 East 196th Street, Noblesville, 46060. Open daily from 8 a.m. to 5 p.m. Admission is free. (317) 776-0779

Children's Museum of Indianapolis, 3000 North Meridian Street, Indianapolis, 46208. Monday through Saturday from 10 a.m. to 3:30 p.m., Sunday from 12:30 p.m. to 3:30 p.m. Admission is $6 for adults, $2 for children ages 2 to 17, and $5 for seniors. (317) 924-5431

Circle Centre Mall, 49 West Maryland Avenue, **Indianapolis**, 46225. Monday through Saturday from 10 a.m. to 9 p.m., Sunday from 10 a.m. to 6 p.m. Parking costs $1 for 3 hours. (317) 681-8000

⚘ **Visitors watch a Gambel's quail at the Indianapolis Zoo**

City Market, 222 East Market Street, Indianapolis, 46204. Monday through Friday from 10 a.m. to 5:30 p.m., Saturday from 10 a.m. to 5 p.m., Sunday from noon to 5 p.m. Admission is free. (317) 634-9266

Commissioner of Agriculture, 402 West Washington Street, Indianapolis, 46204. (317) 232-8770

Conner Prairie, 13400 Allisonville Road, Fishers, 46060. Tuesday through Saturday from 9 a.m. to 5 p.m., Sunday from 11 a.m. to 5 p.m. Prairietown is open from April 3 to November 24. Admission is $9 for adults, $6.50 for children, $8.50 for seniors. (317) 776-6000

Crown Hill Cemetery, 700 West 38th Street, Indianapolis, 46208. Office hours are 8 a.m. to 5 p.m. Guided tours are available for groups of 15 or more. Admission is free. (317) 925-8231

Discovery Zone, 3720 East 82nd Street, Indianapolis, 46250. Monday through Thursday from 11 a.m. to 8 p.m., Friday from 11 a.m. to 10 p.m., Saturday from 10 a.m. to 9 p.m., Sunday from 11 a.m. to 7 p.m. Admission is free for children 1 year and under, $3.99 for children ages 1 to 3, $5.99 for children ages 3 to 12, adults are free when accompanied by a paying child. (317) 577-1565.

Eagle Creek Park, 7840 West 56th Street, Indianapolis, 46254. Hours are dawn until dusk. Admission is $3 per carload up to 5 passengers, 25 cents for each additional passenger. (317) 327-7110

Eiteljorg Museum of American Indians and Western Art, 500 West Washington Street, Indianapolis, 46204. Tuesday through Saturday from 10 a.m. to 5 p.m., Sunday from noon to 5 p.m., closed Thanksgiving, Christmas, and New Year's Day. Admission is $5 for adults, $2 for children ages 5 to 17, free for children under 4, $4 for seniors, and $10 for families. (317) 636-WEST

Greatimes, 5341 Elmwood Ave, Indianapolis, 46237. Monday through Thursday from 11 a.m. to 9 p.m., Friday and Saturday from 11 a.m. to midnight, Sunday from 11 a.m. to 9 p.m. Costs are $4 per game of miniature golf, $4 per ride for Go-Karts and bumper boats, and 50 cents for ten pitches in the batting cage. (317) 780-0300

Gray Brothers Cafeteria, 555 South Indiana Street, Mooresville, 46158. (317) 831-5614

⚘ **A Prairietown villager at Conner Prairie**

Holcomb Observatory, 4600 Sunset Avenue, Indianapolis, 46239. Admission is $2.50 for adults, $1.25 for students, $1 for children. Call for dates and times of shows. (317) 940-9333

Holliday Park, 6349 Spring Mill Road, Indianapolis, 46260. Open dawn until dusk. (317) 327-7180

Hook's American Drugstore Museum, 1180 East 38th Street, Indianapolis, 46205. Open Tuesday through Sunday from 11 a.m. to 5 p.m. Admission is free. (317) 924-1503

Iaria's Italian Restaurant, 317 South College Avenue, Indianapolis, 46202. Lunch served Tuesday through Friday from 11 a.m. to 2 p.m., Dinner served Tuesday through Thursday from 5 p.m. to 9 p.m. and Friday through Saturday from 5 p.m. to 10:30 p.m. (317) 638-7706

IMAX 3D Theater, 650 West Washington Street, Indianapolis, 46204. Admission is $8 for adults, $4.50 for children, $7 for seniors. (317) 233-4629

Indiana Basketball Hall of Fame, One Hall of Fame Court, New Castle, 46362. Tuesday through Saturday from 10 a.m. to 5 p.m., Sunday from 1 p.m. to 5 p.m., closed Monday. Admission is $3 for adults, $1 for children. (765) 529-1891

Indiana Pacers, 300 East Market Street, Indianapolis, 46204. Box office open Monday through Friday from 10 a.m. to 5 p.m. The Pacers play all home games at Market Square Arena. Ticket prices range from $9 to $32. (317) 263-2100

Indiana Pork Producers, 8902 Vincennes Circle, Indianapolis, 46268. (317) 872-7500

Indiana Repertory Theater, 140 West Washington Street, Indianapolis, 46204. Box office open daily from 10 a.m. to 6 p.m. Performances Tuesday through Saturday from September through May. (317) 635-5252

Indiana War Memorial, 431 North Meridian Street, Indianapolis, 46204. Open daily from 8 a.m. to 4:30 p.m. exept on major holidays. Admission is free. (317) 232-7615

Indiana/World Skating Academy, 201 S. Capitol, Indianapolis, 46225. Admission is $3.50 for adults, $2.75 for children under 12. Skate rental is $1.50 for figure skates and $2 for hockey skates. Call for current schedule of dates and times. (317) 237-5555

Indianapolis Ballet Theater, 502-B North Capitol Avenue, Indianapolis, 46204. Administrative offices open weekdays from 9 a.m. to 5 p.m. Admission from $12 to $30. (317) 637-8979

Indianapolis Colts, 7001 West 56th Street, Indianapolis, 46254. The Colts play all of their home games at the RCA Dome. Tickets range from $15 to $40 and are available through TicketMaster or the RCA Dome box office. (317) 297-2658

Indianapolis Ice, 222 East Market Street, Indianapolis, 46204. The Ice, the Chicago Blackhawks farm team, play all home games in Market Square Arena. The season runs from October to April. Tickets range from $9 to $15 and can be purchased through TicketMaster or the MSA box office. (317) 266-1234

Indianapolis Indians, 501 West Maryland Street, Indianapolis, 46225. The Indians, the Cincinnati Reds farm team, play all home games at Victory Field. Their season runs from April to September. Tickets range from $4 to $8. (317) 269-3545

Indianapolis Motor Speedway, 4790 West 16th Street, Speedway, 46222. Tickets for the Indianapolis 500 range from $30 to $140. Tickets for the Brickyard 400 range from $30 to $125. Both races sell out each year. (317) 481-8500

Indianapolis Motor Speedway Hall of Fame Museum, 4790 West 16th Street, Speedway, 46222. The museum is open 364 days a year from 9 a.m. to 5 p.m. Admission is $2 for adults, free for children under 16. Bus tours around the track are $2. (317) 484-6747

Indianapolis Museum of Art, 1200 West 38th Street, Indianapolis, 46208. Tuesday, Wednesday, Friday, and Saturday from 10 a.m. to 5 p.m., Sunday from noon to 5 p.m., closed Mondays. Admission is free except for special exhibits. (317) 923-1331

Indianapolis Parks and Recreation Office, 1426 West 29th Street, Indianapolis, 46208. Information source for Indianapolis' 140 parks and all their programs. (317) 327-0000

Indianapolis Symphony Orchestra, 45 Monument Circle, Indianapolis, 46204. Series subscriptions and single tickets are available for the Classical, Pops, Family, Educational, and Holiday concerts. Tickets range from $12 to $35. (317) 639-4300

Indianapolis Zoo, 1200 West Washington Street, Indianapolis, 46204. Open daily at 9 a.m. Admission is $9 for adults, $5.50 for children ages 3 to 12, $6.50 for seniors. Parking is $3. (317) 630-2030

🔆 **A rippling stream near Indianapolis**

Indy Island, 8575 East Raymond Street, Acton, 46239. Open on Monday, Wednesday, and Friday from 3:30 p.m. to 9 p.m., Saturday and Sunday from noon to 6 p.m. Admission is $4.50 for adults, $3.50 for children, free for children under 2. (317) 862-6867

James Whitcomb Riley Museum Home, 528 Lockerbie Street, Indianapolis, 46202. Tuesday through Saturday from 10 a.m. to 4 p.m., Sunday from noon to 4 p.m. Admission is $2 for adults, 50 cents for children ages 7 to 17, free for children under 6, $1.50 for seniors. (317) 631-5885

Madame Walker Urban Life Center, 617 Indiana Avenue, Indianapolis, 46202. Business office hours are weekdays from 8:30 a.m. to 5 p.m. Call for tour, jazz concert, lecture, and drama information. (317) 236-2088

Major Taylor Velodrome, 3649 Cold Springs Road, Indianapolis, 46208. If weather permits, the velodrome offers open riding at a cost of $2 per rider. Call for schedule of races and open riding dates and times. (317) 926-8356

Old Spaghetti Factory, 210 South Meridian Street, Indianapolis, 46225. Lunch served Monday through Friday from 11:30 a.m. to 4 p.m., Dinner served Monday through Thursday from 4 p.m. to 10 p.m. and Friday and Saturday from 4 p.m. to 11 p.m., Sunday noon 10 p.m. (317) 635-6325

Putt-Putt Golf and Games, 1936 East Southport Road, Indianapolis, 46227. Monday through Friday from 11 a.m. to 10 p.m., Saturday and Sunday from 10 a.m. to 11 p.m. (317) 787-4852

Rathskellar Restaurant, 401 East Michigan Street, Indianapolis, 46204. Lunch served Monday through Friday from 11 a.m. to 2 p.m., Dinner served Tuesday through Thursday from 5:30 p.m. to 9:30 p.m. and Friday and Saturday from 5:30 p.m. to 10 p.m. (317) 636-0396

RCA Dome, 100 South Capitol Street, Indianapolis, 46225. Public tours Monday through Saturday at 11 a.m., 1 p.m., 3 p.m.; Sunday at 1 p.m. and 3 p.m. (except holidays and event days). (317) 262-3663 RollerDome In-line skating is offered from December through March, Monday through Friday from 5 p.m. to 9 p.m., Saturday and Sunday from 1 p.m. to 5 p.m., Holidays Monday through Sunday from 2 p.m. to 9 p.m. Ticket prices $5 for adults, $4 for students, $3 for pre-teens. (317) 824-DOME

Rick's Cafe Boatyard, 4050 Dandy Trail, Indianapolis, 46254. Lunch served Monday through Saturday from 11 a.m. to 4 p.m., Dinner served Sunday through Thursday from 4 p.m. to 11 p.m. and Friday and Saturday from 4 p.m. to midnight. (317) 290-9300

Shaffer's Restaurant, 6125 Hillside Avenue, Indianapolis, 46220. Dinner served Monday through Thursday from 5 p.m. to 9 p.m., Friday and Saturday from 5 p.m. to 11 p.m., Sunday from 4 p.m. to 9 p.m. (317) 253-1404

Shapiro's Delicatessan, 808 South Meridian Street, Indianapolis, 46225. Breakfast served daily from 6:30 a.m. to 11 a.m., lunch from 11 a.m. to 4 p.m., dinner served 4 p.m. to 8:30 p.m. (317) 631-4041

Sitzmark, 930 South Range Line Road, Carmel, 46032. Monday through Friday from 10 a.m. to 8 p.m., Saturday from 10 a.m. to 6 p.m., Sunday from noon to 5 p.m. Cost for skate rental (skates, pads, and helmet) is $10 for a day, $15 overnight, and $28 for a weekend. (317) 844-8222

Soldiers' and Sailors' Monument, Monument Circle. Open 7 days a week from 10 a.m. to 7 p.m. Admission is free. (317) 232-7615

Stonycreek Farm, 11366 State Road 38 East, Noblesville, 46060. Monday through Friday from 10 a.m. to 5 p.m., Saturday and Sunday from 10 a.m. to 5 p.m. Admission on weekends is $2 for kids ages 16 or older, free for kids 15 and under. No charge during the week. (317) 776-9930

⇑ **The Bumping Bullfrog ride at the Indianapolis Zoo**

Union Station, 39 Jackson Place South Drive, Indianapolis, 46225. Hours are Monday through Thursday from 10 a.m. to 9 p.m., Friday and Saturday from 10 a.m. to 10 p.m., Sunday from 11 a.m. to 6 p.m. Admission is free. (317) 267-0700

Wolf Park, 4004 East 800 North, Battle Ground, 47920. May until November open daily from 1 p.m. to 5 p.m. Special "Howl Nights" every Friday and Saturday starting at 7:30 p.m. From December to April "Howl Nights" only on Saturday at 7:30 p.m. Closed major holidays. Admission is $4 for ages 14 and up, free for children age 13 and under. On Sundays, admission is $5 for ages 14 and up, free for children age 13 and under. (765) 567-2265

ANSWERS TO PUZZLES

page 5

```
M H E L I C O P T E R R L F O
O O U C H D P W T O P G Y K G
T O R C A R R M O S R M F I B M O
T O R T A I R P L A N E A S B L
R C B P L D R S W H B T L T K B
C O B T T S T A N M R P N E I
Y A N C R A A G O N O O G T J
C T T H C A C O R U L G Y E L
L L F E C C I N U C L T O W H
E M Y R U K L N L A E U A S S
U I S S B I K E W E Y E L E T
Y U A R H E J B A D K I M Y K
```

page 15

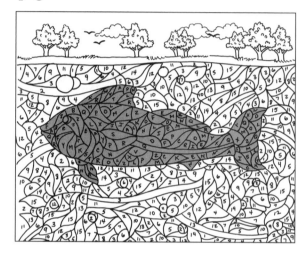

page 19

page 17

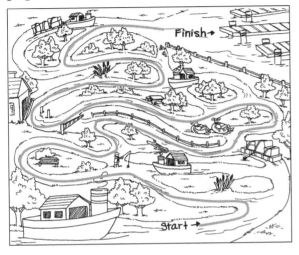

page 21

page 23

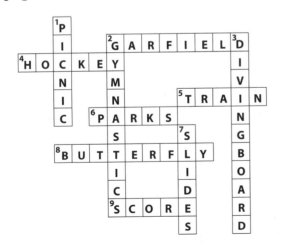

page 25

page 33

W	A	L	X	S	J	Y	Q	G	J	X	G	J	U	W	F	J
N	L	G	W	L	K	Q	F	B	Y	J	L	X	K	U	Q	L
K	W	R	F	Q	X	L	K	N	K	F	X	Q	Q	X	W	Y
Q	J	K	W	F	L	E	G	X	K	L	G	D	Y	L	L	X
F	L	X	K	Z	F	L	W	L	E	G	F	X	G	W	L	G
Y	L	K	W	X	F	B	W	F	K	X	R	W	F	Q	A	Y

Answer: A SUNBURNED ZEBRA

page 35

K	O	B	A	Q	K	M	E	W	O	P	M	E	G	G	S	H
W	P	L	E	R	D	Q	R	Y	M	H	E	B	T	O	N	H
I	Y	U	Y	S	U	O	I	N	N	P	T	S	P	A	T	F
N	A	E	S	H	U	M	M	I	N	G	B	I	R	D	U	D
G	J	J	F	G	M	N	H	D	V	C	E	N	O	J	D	N
D	C	A	R	D	I	N	A	L	N	N	O	K	B	S	E	Y
E	D	Y	Z	G	X	N	N	C	U	I	U	Y	I	V	W	R
O	B	N	Q	P	T	I	N	M	K	C	K	M	N	Q	N	W
R	W	E	G	T	R	R	H	K	F	A	M	W	Z	C	E	T
U	I	L	E	I	E	U	R	N	E	Y	D	R	V	I	S	B
R	O	T	B	L	E	E	T	B	U	L	I	E	Y	N	T	B
S	E	A	G	U	L	L	Y	F	O	C	O	N	K	E		

page 37

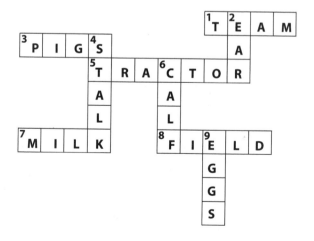

page 41

Across/Down crossword solution:

1 TEAM
3 PIGS
5 TRACTOR
7 MILK
8 FIELD

Down: 2 EAR / 4 STALL / 6 CAL / 9 EGGS

page 47

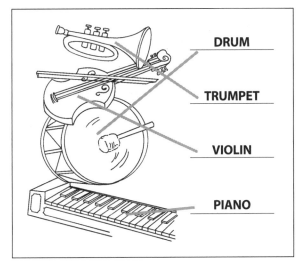

DRUM

TRUMPET

VIOLIN

PIANO

page 49

```
A S T Q M S E C D R P H D I N C M
G A H O R N O L E T N K D B J O Z
L B T U O V E N K L F V G S N C K
L A M N M S B A K F L I I X K D T
A S W S S U L T S P O O O V F U O
F S O A Q T R W D R U M L H I C D
I Q R R P S H D R B N M I E T T Z
D W T R O M B O N E M O N N E O A
C L A R I N E T T A D B M X N R A
O F W D X D G U E L C S M X E W L
X Q I N S S L J W L S X K D U F I
H J S L N F Y B I N M U S I C S L
```

page 51

page 53

page 61

page 65

page 77

page 79

page 81

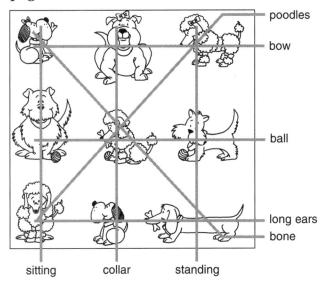

poodles
bow
ball
long ears
bone

sitting   collar   standing

page 83

page 85

page 93

```
C U G E W L S S G N X (S T R I K E)
H A H B R D Q S Y L H E B A E N H
N Y N A S G P I N N A T S A X T F
T T A L L E Y E G T K N G D R P D
R R T L G K R R D V U E E O E I N
X E R U V M A M N G N S S G S G N Y
E E S S P U N N H U G C Y O B S R
S T A S P E I N D K C O M H D D W
I U R C U K G U T T E R G F J Q T
U R S E I S U R N N Y E N L M U B
R N T B L S R T U U L X B Y N F S
D Y D N I O F Y H (S H O E S) E Q R
```

page 97

page 99

page 105

page 107

page 109

page 111

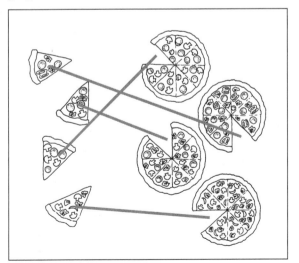

page 113

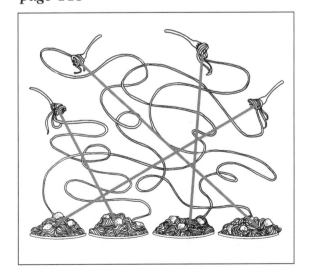

GEOGRAPHICAL INDEX: WHERE IS EVERYTHING?

Northeast Indianapolis
Bazbeaux's Pizza
Broad Ripple Ducks
City Market
Hook's American Drugstore
Indiana Pacers
Indiana War Memorial
Indianapolis Symphony Orchestra
Monon Trail
Monument Circle
Rathskellar
Riley Home Museum
Soldiers' and Sailor's Monument
Shaffer's Restaurant

Northwest Indianapolis
Acapulco Joe's
Children's Museum of Indianapolis
Circle Centre Mall
Crown Hill Cemetery
Eagle Creek Park
Eiteljorg Museum
Holcomb Observatory
Holliday Park
Imax 3D Theater
Indianapolis Motor Speedway
Indianapolis Water Company Canal
Indianapolis Zoo
Major Taylor Velodrome
Rick's Cafe Boatyard

Southwest Indianapolis
Indiana/World Skating Academy
RCA Dome
River Promenade
Shapiro's Delicatessan
The Old Spaghetti Factory
Victory Field

Southeast Indianapolis
Action Bowl
Adrian Orchard
Greatimes
Iaria's Restaurant
Indy Island

Greater Indianapolis
Canterbury Arabians
Conner Prairie
Gray Brother's Cafeteria
Stonycreek Farm
Wolf Park

INDEX

from John Muir Publications

American Origins Series
Each is 48 pages and $12.95 hardcover.

Tracing Our English Roots
Tracing Our German Roots
Tracing Our Irish Roots
Tracing Our Italian Roots
Tracing Our Japanese Roots
Tracing Our Jewish Roots
Tracing Our Polish Roots

Bizarre & Beautiful Series
Each is 48 pages, $14.95 hardcover, $9.95 paperback.

Bizarre & Beautiful Ears
Bizarre & Beautiful Eyes
Bizarre & Beautiful Feelers
Bizarre & Beautiful Noses
Bizarre & Beautiful Tongues

Extremely Weird Series
Each is 32 pages and $5.95 paperback.

Extremely Weird Animal Defenses
Extremely Weird Animal Disguises
Extremely Weird Animal Hunters
Extremely Weird Bats
Extremely Weird Endangered Species
Extremely Weird Fishes
Extremely Weird Frogs
Extremely Weird Reptiles
Extremely Weird Spiders
Extremely Weird Birds
Extremely Weird Insects

Extremely Weird Mammals
Extremely Weird Micro Monsters
Extremely Weird Primates
Extremely Weird Sea Creatures
Extremely Weird Snakes

Kidding Around® Series
Each is 144 pages and $7.95 paperback.

Kidding Around Atlanta
Kidding Around Cleveland
Kids Go! Denver
Kidding Around Indianapolis
Kidding Around Minneapolis/St. Paul
Kidding Around San Francisco
Kids Go! Seattle
Kidding Around Washington, D.C.

Kids Explore Series
Written by kids for kids, each is $9.95 paperback.

Kids Explore America's African American Heritage, 160 pages
Kids Explore America's Hispanic Heritage, 160 pages
Kids Explore America's Japanese American Heritage, 160 pages
Kids Explore America's Jewish Heritage, 160 pages
Kids Explore the Gifts of Children with Special Needs, 128 pages
Kids Explore the Heritage of Western Native Americans, 128 pages